"In a couple of my books, I  is both easy to understand and him *really* easy to understand ¿

PETER KREEFT
Author of *Summa of the Summa*, *A Shorter Summa*,
and *Practical Theology*

"Even many Catholics probably imagine that the ideas of St. Thomas Aquinas could only be of interest or understandable to theologians, philosophers, and other intellectuals. Nothing could be further from the truth, as Matt Fradd shows. This engaging book conveys the wisdom of the Angelic Doctor in a way that is accessible, practical, and witty."

EDWARD FESER
Professor of Philosophy, Pasadena City College

"The pursuit of happiness didn't get underway with Thomas Jefferson or the pop psychology publishing industry of the twentieth century or the intriguing findings of the neurosciences in the twenty-first. The question of what makes human beings happy depends upon knowing what human beings are for. In pursuit of these questions, Fradd heeds the guidance of many wise and, I presume, happy minds—chief of which is Thomas Aquinas, who was called the Angelic Doctor for good reason. Find out why. Your happiness depends on it."

AL KRESTA
President and CEO of Ave Maria Radio and
Host of "Kresta in the Afternoon"

"This book brims with good sense and persuasive reasoning. Every chapter is an instruction manual for how to live well. Yet, what sets this marvelous book apart is its reminder—through Fradd's stories about his own life— that happiness, in the fullness that we seek, is elusive in this broken world and, besides, we too often find ourselves in a mess. In such circumstances, is the hope of happiness gone? On the contrary, Fradd invites us to throw ourselves upon the greatness of the mercy of God and to discover happiness precisely in the immensity of divine grace. Here we encounter the life of virtue at its source."

MATTHEW LEVERING
James N. and Mary D. Perry Jr. Chair of Theology,
Mundelein Seminary

"St. Thomas Aquinas is known for his towering intellect, but his incredibly down-to-earth wisdom about how to find happiness is accessible to all. In this short book, Matt Fradd presents the Angelic Doctor's roadmap to joy, which includes relaxing baths, growth in virtue, how to master our emotions, and more!"

JASON EVERT
Founder of the Chastity Project

"People, in general, no longer see the path of faith and virtue as the path to happiness. People are also more miserable than ever. Matt Fradd brings the wisdom of Aquinas to life like no one else. And in a world losing its way in the quest for fulfillment, we need that wisdom now more than ever. This is a must read and a must share."

CHRIS STEFANICK
President of Real Life Catholic and Author of *Living Joy*

"Matt Fradd continues to do the Church and the world an immense service by distilling the thought of St. Thomas Aquinas and showcasing his contemporary relevance for the questions besetting modern man—e.g., questions regarding God, happiness, and overcoming the pull of sadness. The reader encounters here not only the Angelic Doctor but also benefits tremendously from the wit and insight of Matt Fradd, who has become one of the most important Catholic voices today. I highly recommend this book!"

ANDREW SWAFFORD
Associate Professor, Benedictine College, and author and host of
Hebrews: The New and Eternal Covenant

HOW TO BE HAPPY

HOW TO BE HAPPY

SAINT THOMAS'
SECRET TO A GOOD LIFE

MATT FRADD

EMMAUS
ROAD
PUBLISHING

Steubenville, Ohio
www.emmausroad.org

Emmaus Road Publishing
1468 Parkview Circle
Steubenville, Ohio 43952

©2021 Matt Fradd
All rights reserved. Published 2021
Printed in the United States of America
Second Printing 2021

Library of Congress Control Number 2021936217
ISBN 978-1-64585-131-8 paperback / 978-1-64585-132-5 ebook

Cover design and layout by Emily Demary
Cover image: *The Chastity of St. Thomas*. Photo by Fr. Lawrence, O.P., via Flickr.

To my very good wife, Cameron, who, upon learning during one of my rather dramatic, melancholic, moody spells that I had written a book entitled How to be Happy, *said, "Wow, you should read that!"*

TABLE OF CONTENTS

FOREWORD   xi

SECTION 1: OUR TRUE END   1

   1. God, the Universe, and Everything   3
   2. Meet St. Thomas Aquinas   15
   3. Aquinas on God and Happiness   25

SECTION 2: WHAT WILL *NOT* MAKE US HAPPY   33

   4. Can Sin Make Me Happy?   35
   5. Can Bodily Pleasures Make Me Happy?   49
   6. Can Interior Pleasures Make Me Happy?   61

SECTION 3: WHAT *WILL* MAKE US HAPPY   73

   7. Prudent "Moral Muscles"   75
   8. Temperate, Just Courage   85
   9. Faith, Hope, and Love   93

SECTION 4: GROUNDING OUR HAPPINESS   103

   10. Controlling Our Passions   105
   11. What to Do When Life Hurts   115
   12. How Scruples Steal Happiness   125

CONCLUSION: HAPPINESS, WITH A
LITTLE HELP FROM AQUINAS   137

FOREWORD

IT'S LEGITIMATE FOR PEOPLE TO ASK what medieval philosophy can possibly have to do with happiness. Etymologically, *philosophy* means "the love of wisdom." But historically it has come to represent an academic field remote from the experience or interest of ordinary people. And wouldn't "medieval" only make it worse—make it even more irrelevant?

I must confess that we Thomists—we who profess to follow Aquinas—can sometimes confirm these dire suspicions. In our zeal for the Master's logic, we fail to communicate his sense of wonder, his passion for truth, and his grounding in Scripture. We edit out the very elements that might make him attractive to students and other amateurs. What we're left with are lines of Latin that are lackluster by the Master's design.

It takes a true genius to convey the excitement contained in Thomas' precisions. Chesterton was such a genius. His little biography, *The Dumb Ox*, left the great philosopher Étienne Gilson awestruck and envious to the end of his days. Chesterton did what professionals considered impossible—or beneath their dignity. He made the reading of medieval philosophy as rewarding and entertaining as anything in the morning papers. Gilson, endorsing *The Dumb Ox*, marveled over Chesterton's little volume: "I consider it as being, without possible comparison, the best book ever written on Saint Thomas . . . [T]he few readers who have spent twenty or thirty years in studying St. Thomas Aquinas, and who, perhaps, have themselves published two or three volumes on the subject, cannot fail to perceive that the so-called 'wit' of Chesterton has put their scholarship to shame."

Chesterton was such a genius. Matt Fradd is another such genius. Some years ago, he took up the seemingly quixotic task of launching a podcast on the perennial philosophy. He called it *Pints with Aquinas*. I'm sure some philosophers smirked. They *knew* that Aquinas should be left to professionals and kept out of earbuds. What could podcast listeners glean from the Angelic Doctor in their few minutes of mediated listening per day?

They can gain happiness. Matt Fradd knew that, as Josef Pieper knew it when he wrote *Happiness and Contemplation*. And Chesterton knew it before both of them.

Matt succeeded at his podcast—and he succeeds in this book—because St. Thomas Aquinas wasn't an otherworldly nerd consumed by questions of inhuman abstraction. Thomas was a philosopher at a time when the word was true to its roots. He was a philosopher as passionate as Plato, Boethius, Pascal, and Kierkegaard. No one accuses those men of being bloodless or dull. They were on a high-stakes adventure, and so was Thomas.

It wasn't a quirky academic interest that consumed him. It was the longing for happiness. It was a desire he knew he shared with every blacksmith and seamstress and stable boy in the city of Paris in the middle of the thirteenth century.

He shares it with us today, every single one of us.

This explains the success of Matt Fradd's podcast. He gets what many professors have forgotten. He remembers the first thrill of discovery on reading Thomas, and he communicates that thrill in a way everyone can understand.

It will astonish some readers that this book is structured entirely upon the pursuit of happiness. They don't associate that endeavor with Aquinas. They don't even associate it with Christianity. But that only goes to show how far we've drifted from our origins and our medieval moorings.

We think in post-Reformation terms. We think of morality as based on law and commands. But for Aquinas, as for Jesus and St. Paul, it was based on love and virtue. Law has its place in Christian thought and life, and we need commandments. But even these have to be understood in the context of happiness. The God who created us wants us to be happy, not just at some undisclosed time in the distant future. He wants us to be happy now, and his commands show us how to be happy. He never commands what he does not enable us to do.

So many people today think "happiness" is synonymous with "pleasure." Yet no one grows happy from a superabundance of pleasure. They grow jaded and burned out. They pursue pleasure as an end, and it destroys them.

During the Second World War, my father served as an assistant to General Douglas MacArthur. The Big Chief once told my dad about the liberation of the Philippines—how soldiers parched from the heat would rush toward salt water to slake their maddening thirst. They had to be stopped by force. They saw water as the obvious relief for their misery, but that particular water would only make them more miserable and bring them to a painful death.

So many people today are like those soldiers. So many people want happiness, but pursue joyless pleasures instead.

In this book we can see the happiness that's true—and we can also sense the joy that comes with it, the joy that only comes with virtue and sacrificial love.

This is the only wisdom that's truly lovable.

Scott Hahn

SECTION 1

OUR TRUE END

1.

GOD, THE UNIVERSE, AND EVERYTHING

WHEN I WAS ABOUT TWELVE YEARS OLD, I had a good friend of the same age whom I'll call Jane. Like me, Jane enjoyed pondering deep questions. One day she wanted to go rollerblading and after a while we pulled over to the side of the road and she began telling me about a bunch of negative things going on in her life. At one point she said something for which I had no response.

"Matt, I don't know why I should continue to go on living."

As a twelve-year-old who was still figuring out how to roller blade without looking like a dork (and not succeeding) I just thought to myself, "What do I have to say to this girl?" But she continued, "Can you give me a reason? One will do."

I was concerned that Jane asked this but I didn't think she was on the verge of killing herself. It felt more like Jane was stuck on a question a lot of other people don't think about. What's the point of this life?

I didn't have a religious answer for Jane because at this stage of my life I wasn't sure that God existed. I wouldn't have said I

3

was an atheist back then, but I was an agnostic, probably. God, I was beginning to think, was something we liked to believe because we didn't like the idea of death, of never seeing our loved ones again, of life having no ultimate purpose. And here was the problem. If life had no ultimate purpose, and Jane was asking me for a purpose to go on living, then what could I say?

"But Jane, you're awesome . . ."

She looked at me as if to say, "Seriously? That's all you got."

The answer had to be a little deeper. I continued: "Well look, next year we go to high school—which will be awesome."

"Yeah. I guess. Then what?"

"Well, we'll graduate high school. You can go to university if you want and then you'll get married and have kids and that'll be great."

"Yeah. I guess. Then what?"

I took a breath and gave in.

"Well, then you'll die. I guess everyone has to die." She looked at me as if to say, "Do you see my point?" It pierced me because I did see her point, that if this is the outcome of our life, if we just all end in death, why continue going on? Especially when life is inconvenient or if you're suffering, why bother?

THE PURSUIT OF HAPPINESS

Blaise Pascal said that there are three types of people in the world. There are those who have sought the truth about God and have found it. There are those who are seeking the truth about God but have not yet found it. Then there are those who neither seek nor find God.

The first group is wise because they knew to seek God and are happy because they have now found him. The second group is wise because they knew to seek God, but they are unhappy because they have not yet found him. Of the third group Pascal said, "I have no words to describe so silly a creature."[1]

But someone might ask, "Can't a person lead a good and happy life without God? Is it silly to believe you can be happy in this life even if you're not religious?" I used to belong to that third group of people, so I appreciate that Pascal tried to get inside their heads. This is what he said they must tell themselves to justify their indifference:

> I see only infinity on every side hemming me in like an atom or like the shadow of a fleeting instant. All I know is that I must soon die, but what I know least about is this very death which I cannot evade.... And my conclusion from all this is that I must pass my days without a thought of seeking what is to happen to me.... I will go without fear or foresight to face so momentous an event, and allow myself to be carried off limply to my death, uncertain of my future state for all eternity.[2]

Or as the 1988 one-hit wonder Bobby McFerrin put it: "Don't worry, be happy." In other words, this third group of people would say to Pascal, "Look, you know you've got this life now, so make the best of it. Just be try to be happy before the timer runs out."

---

[1] Blaise Pascal, *Pensées*, trans. A. J. Krailsheimer (New York: Penguin Books, 1995), §194.

[2] Pascal, *Pensées*, §130.

But for many of us happiness is like the horizon: the more we chase it, the more it seems to be that much further away, no matter how long and fast we run.

That's because happiness isn't a *thing* we can locate and store away like other goods. For example, if you want to be wealthy, you just have to find a way to acquire lots of money. If you want to be educated, you can collect knowledge at school or in books. But you can't just go to a store, bank, or library and pick up some "happiness" to take home with you.

The American politician William Bennett provided the perfect description of what it's like to try and "find" happiness: "Happiness is like a cat. If you try to coax it or call it, it will avoid you; it will never come. But if you pay no attention to it and go about your business, you'll find it rubbing against your legs and jumping into your lap."

In America we talk about "the pursuit of happiness," but the famous psychologist and Nazi-concentration-camp survivor Viktor Frankl once said, "Happiness cannot be pursued; it must ensue. One must have a reason to 'be happy.'"[3] Frankl then compared happiness to laughter, noting that you can't make someone laugh by saying, "Hey buddy, cheer up and have a laugh." They might pretend to laugh but it's always a fake laugh. Real, joyful laughter has to come from a *reason* to find something funny, and Frankl recognized (in a treatment he called "logotherapy") that happiness is rooted in finding the reason we should be happy.

That's exactly what Jane and so many other people are seeking: a reason to be happy. And when people offer them various

---

[3] Viktor Frankl, *Man's Search for Meaning* (Boston: Beacon Press, 1992), 140.

reasons based on the shifting, temporary things in this life, they aren't impressed. It might make you happy now, but what happens when the winds of life change and things start to fall apart, as they always do at some point?

UNENDING HAPPINESS

And not only do we want something that doesn't exist as a thing we can easily grasp; we want our happiness to never end.

In Jonathan Swift's novel *Gulliver's Travels*, the title character meets a group of people called the Struldbrugs, who are born with red dots on their foreheads, which indicate that they will never die. "Happy nation, where every child hath at least a chance for being immortal!" Gulliver exclaims.

Unlike other non-human animals, we worry about death when it's not staring us in the face and we desire a happy life that never ends. Three hundred years after Swift wrote *Gulliver's Travels*, scientists and tech moguls are using the latest in gene editing and computer technology to extend life and possibly make people immortal. An author in *The New Yorker* writes that for these researchers, "death would no longer be a metaphysical problem, merely a technical one."[4]

But think about this for a moment: isn't it weird to have a deep, unyielding desire for the impossible?

If you saw me fretting about not having enough food to eat or a decent place to sleep at night, you'd understand. There are ways to get people good food and a comfortable roof over

---

[4] Tad Friend, "Silicon Valley's Quest to Live Forever," *The New Yorker*, April 3, 2017. Available online at https://www.newyorker.com/magazine/2017/04/03/silicon-valleys-quest-to-live-forever.

their heads. But if you saw me freaking out over the fact that I can't fly by simply flapping my arms, you'd think I'd gone slightly crazy. "Matt, people aren't able to do these things, so why are you upset that you can't do them?"

Of course, there may be a few people who desire the impossible, but it would be odd if everyone desired something that could never be satisfied. The Christian author C. S. Lewis once said this about our desires:

> Creatures are not born with desires unless satisfaction for these desires exists. A baby feels hunger: well, there is such a thing as food. A duckling wants to swim: well, there is such a thing as water. Men feel sexual desire: well, there is such a thing as sex. If I find in myself a desire which no experience in this world can satisfy, the most probable explanation is that I was made for another world.[5]

Interestingly, a global 2019 survey revealed that actively religious people are happier than people who are not religious.[6] For example, in the United States 36 percent of actively religious people say they are "very happy" compared to 25 percent of religiously unaffiliated people. You find this same "happiness gap" in every other part of the world, including Japan, Germany, Peru, and my home country of Australia. Back home 45 percent of actively religious people say they're "very happy," whereas only 32 percent of religiously unaffiliated people say the same thing.

---

[5] C. S. Lewis, *Mere Christianity* (New York: Harper One, 1980), 136–137.

[6] Joey Marshall, "Are Religious People Happier, Healthier? Our New Global Study Explores This Question," *Pew Research Center*, January 31, 2019. Available online at https://www.pewresearch.org/fact-tank/2019/01/31/are-religious-people-happier-healthier-our-new-global-study-explores-this-question/.

Now, please don't misunderstand the point I'm making.

I think it's false to say that if you merely choose to go to church then you'll be happy. There are plenty of unhappy people sitting in the pews and no doubt happy non-religious people. But I also think it would be foolish to ignore the evidence that shows our happiness is not found solely in this life and that we have to look deeper to find out what will make us truly happy.

Karl Marx once said that religion was "the opiate of the masses." From his perspective, religion only keeps people happy by dulling their pain and blinding them to misery in this life. However, in my journey of faith the opposite happened—I got a new perspective that showed me how true happiness comes from seeing the world as it really is.

ON THE PATH TO RELIGION

My mum was Catholic and took me and my siblings to Holy Mass every week. My dad wasn't (but later converted). I had stopped going to Holy Mass whenever I could wear Mum down enough to the point where she'd say, "Okay, fine, you can stay home, but you're coming next week."

One day Mum came home and said to me, "Matthew, there's this lady who was at church tonight, and she spoke about this trip, this pilgrimage thing called World Youth Day. There's going to be a couple of million people there and the pope's going to come too."

At first I thought it was a trick. It sounded far too good to be true. Perhaps, I thought, Rome was the name of an obscure little town in South Australia—population thirty-two or something. "Rome? Like . . . Like, Rome, Italy?" I said.

"Do you know any other Rome?" she said.

"Will there be girls?" I asked.

My mum was talking about an international gathering of Catholic young people taking place in Rome called World Youth Day. She graciously paid for me to attend, hoping it would jumpstart a religious experience. But she did give me this warning: "Now Matthew, I'm not paying all this money for you to go over there and make a bloody idiot of yourself." Fair point. If you had known me back then, you'd put dibs on "making an idiot of himself" over "comes to Jesus." I promised Mum I wouldn't and we began planning the trip.

Up until this point the only Christians I had met were awkward evangelists who seemed like they were trying to sell me something. One time a group of them was offering free hot dogs at a place we liked to hang out called The Boat Ramp.

I remember we'd be standing around going, "Okay, we got to get in there, get the hot dogs, and get out."

"But you know they're going to talk to us about Jesus," one of my mates answered.

"I know, but I'm really hungry. Okay, here we go. One, two, three, go!"

They were the sorts of Christians that were so happy, it made you sick. "G'Day mate," they said, far too enthusiastically. "How are you doing? You okay? Hotdog?"

"Yes, please," I said, trying not to make eye contact.

At some point—I think this only happened to me once— someone said, "Mate, do you go to church, do you?" I said,

"Not really. Kind of. I used to." I remember this bloke; I can still recall his face.

He said, "Have you accepted Jesus Christ as your personal Lord and Savior?" Looking back, I wish I had said, "No, but I'll accept a hotdog." Man, that would have been good.

Now, forgive me if I'm coming down too hard on these happy Christians. I'm sure they were great people and I was just an angsty teenager, but it really did bother me, the way some Christians would do this. It felt like they didn't really care about me; they just wanted to feel good about making another disciple or something.

On my way to Rome the plane stopped in Sydney and it was there that I met, for the first time in my life, young Catholic Christians who believed in Jesus Christ, the Bible, and the teachings of the Catholic Church. And here's the thing. They didn't strike me as weird. On the contrary they were intelligent, cool, good looking. It was their joy that struck me the most. These people went to church, were saving sex until marriage, didn't get drunk or high, yet they were happy.

I wasn't happy. If you had asked me if I was happy, I would have said yes, but I really wasn't. I remember as a teenager when I'd come home from parties and lie in my bed. I hated the silence before drifting off to sleep because I didn't like being alone with my thoughts.

I was terrified. Terrified that deep down something was wrong with me, and that at any moment it would be discovered and I'd be rejected. I think many people feel like this, though they don't have the words to describe it. I certainly didn't at the time. I felt I was broken and unacceptable—and so I had to put on a front, had to make you like me, and I felt good about myself to the degree I was successful at that. These people on the plane with me seemed more raw, more free to be themselves.

But these people weren't sarcastic and they weren't cutting anyone else down. Their success in life didn't depend on anyone else's failure. They were just really genuine, and that was disarming. You can't make fun of somebody—well, not for very long—who's just kind and intelligent. On the long flight from Sydney to Rome I sat next to a bloke who was an actor in Australia (he was once the roommate of the late Heath Ledger).

Once I found that out, I asked, "So you're obviously not going to this World Youth Day thing, right?"

"No, I'm going to World Youth Day as well."

I said, "What, you believe in God?"

He replied, "Yeah, absolutely—I'm Catholic. You don't?"

I wish I could go back in time and slap the seventeen-year-old out of me because I just said something cliché like, "I don't know. I believe everybody needs something to believe in."

I wouldn't have blamed him if he had shot back, "Oh, Confucius, you blew my mind with that statement." But he didn't mock me. Instead he shared with me about how when he was hooked on drugs, a friend invited him to a church where people prayed over him and he's been drug free ever since.

Since my Discman was out of batteries and we had twenty hours to go, we just chatted about all sorts of things related to faith and philosophy. Over the course of that trip I found that these people were intelligent. They believed what the Catholic Church taught, and they knew why they believed what the

Church taught. They weren't just little robots that did what the pope programmed them to do.

When I was there, I remember praying what was perhaps the most sincere prayer I've ever prayed. It went something like this: *God, I don't know if you exist. I'm probably just speaking to myself right now. But if you do, would you reveal yourself to me in a way that I would understand?*

A NEW PERSPECTIVE

Over the next few months I read and prayed and it seemed like a whole new world opened up for me. But rather than tell you what happened, I'd like to show you what happened.

I would like you to raise your right hand up in the air. Go on. Hold this book in one hand and raise up your other hand. Just hold your right hand up in the air. I want you to get your index finger, the one next to the thumb, and point that at the ceiling. Now, make a clockwise circle and make sure it's *clockwise*. As your hand is rotating and drawing this circle on the celling, I want you to bring your hand down past your forehead. Now, past your nose. Keep going clockwise under your chin. Now look down and see which way is your finger going.

Counterclockwise. Amazing, right?

What changed?

Well, you got a new perspective. The same thing appeared completely different because you looked at it in a different way. For me, prayer and worship of God went from being something people did to make themselves feel better (like journaling to a fictional character) to being a way to reconnect to the ultimate source of our fulfillment as human beings.

Even if you're not religious, I hope you'll at least take a moment to look at the question of happiness from this new perspective.

This book isn't about Matt Fradd's tips to be happy. God forbid! I've tried the usual routes to happiness, and you probably have too: popularity, pleasure, margaritas on a beach—okay, that one came close. It also isn't about what self-help authors, gurus, or even respected social scientists say is the key to happiness. Everyone thinks they have an answer to this question, and many of them are correct on at least a few of the things that bring us happiness.

Instead, it's about how one of the most famous thinkers in history, Thomas Aquinas, says we can find happiness. And when you find out a little more about him, I think you'll see that, no matter what you think about God or faith, you'll see that he has some pretty worthwhile things to say.

2.

MEET ST. THOMAS AQUINAS

IF YOU KNOW ANYTHING ABOUT CATHOLICISM, you know that saints are a big deal. Most churches are named after a saint and there are "patron saints," or people in heaven who devote prayers to special causes, for almost everything. (Saint Brigid of Ireland was reputed to have changed water into beer for a group of helpless lepers, thus making her one of the patron saints of beer and of my podcast, *Pints With Aquinas*!)

There are over ten thousand officially canonized saints and millions more whom we've never heard about (the Church celebrates their lives every year on November 1, All Saints Day). But as of today, only thirty-six of them are given the title "Doctor of the Church" because of their extensive contribution to the Church's teachings. One of them is St. Thomas Aquinas, who lived between 1225 and 1274 and was given the title "Angelic Doctor" in 1567. In 1879 Pope Leo XIII said, "Among the Scholastic Doctors, the chief and master of all towers Thomas Aquinas, who, as [Cardinal] Cajetan observes, because 'he most venerated the ancient doctors of the Church, in a certain way seems to have inherited the intellect of all.'"[1] But if you were going to take a doctor's advice, you'd want to see his credentials right? In the case of St. Thomas Aquinas I don't think you'll be disappointed.

THE LIFE OF A "DUMB OX"

Thomas was born in Roccasecca, Italy, and his parents hoped that he would become a Benedictine monk and eventually abbot at Monte Cassino, a position which at the time yielded significant ecclesiastical and political power. But Thomas had his eyes set on joining a new religious order, called the Dominicans, that traveled from town to town, where they preached and depended on donations to sustain them. At one point, his mother had Thomas' brothers kidnap him before the Dominicans could send him to Paris to study. They imprisoned him in the family castle for a year in order to break his holy resolve (his parents liked the job security that came with being a monk and weren't too concerned with the religious aspects of that lifestyle).

His brothers even let a prostitute into his room one night and shut the door, but St. Thomas didn't waste a moment. He went right to the fireplace, where he grabbed a hot iron that was lying in there, and he chased her out of the room. He made a black cross on the back of the door and prayed, after which angels came to visit and strengthened him. From that point on, Thomas was never tempted again to the sin of unchastity.

He later escaped the family castle (though his mother probably let him escape, seeing that he would never change his mind)

---

[1] Leo XIII, *Aeterni Patris* (1879), §17

and went on to study at the University of Paris. St. Thomas didn't speak much and his portly size led many of his fellow students to mock him as "the dumb ox." Albertus Magnus, who would go on to be St. Albert the Great, was one of Thomas' teachers and prophetically said this about him: "You call him a Dumb Ox; I tell you this Dumb Ox shall bellow so loud that his bellowings will fill the world."[2]

In fact, three hundred years later, Pope Pius V declared St. Thomas a Doctor of the Church and said that Thomas was "the most brilliant light of the church." Pope Leo XIII said that even heretics admitted that "if the teaching of Thomas Aquinas were only taken away, they could easily battle with all Catholic teachers, gain the victory, and abolish the Church."[3]

In the modern era Pope St. John Paul II said that "the Church has been justified in consistently proposing Saint Thomas as a master of thought and a model of the right way to do theology."[4] According to Pope Benedict XVI, Aquinas is called "The Angelic Doctor" because of "his virtues, in particular the loftiness of his thought and purity of life." In fact, Aquinas is cited more than almost any other saint in the *Catechism of the Catholic Church*, which contains all the teachings of the Catholic Church (St. Augustine, the Doctor of Grace, comes in at number one).[5]

While he didn't utter many words in casual conversation, Aquinas could dictate to four secretaries on four different subjects all at the same time. One of his works, the *Summa*

---

[2] G. K. Chesterton, *St. Thomas Aquinas* (Mineola, NY: Dover, 2009), 39

[3] Leo XIII, *Aeterni Patris*, §23.

[4] John Paul II, *Fides et Ratio* (1998), §43.

[5] Zenit.org, "On St. Thomas Aquinas," June 2, 2010, https://zenit.org/articles/on-st-thomas-aquinas/.

Theologiae (also called the *Summa Theologica*) sits on my desk in five volumes and is over four thousand pages long. But it's not just a rambling collection of theological babble. It's not easy to read in the same sense that a good medical or engineering textbook isn't easy to read if you don't know the basic vocabulary being used.

But Thomas hated the many rambling theological texts of his time, so he definitely didn't want his work to join their ranks. In the Middle Ages, students would read ancient philosophers like Aristotle or earlier medieval commenters like Boethius, but they did so in a scattered way that focused on rote memorization. Education didn't focus as much on synthesis, or putting all of these teachings together into a unified set of beliefs or critiquing these thinkers in order to make their arguments better. And that's where St. Thomas comes in because, as Pope Leo XIII says of these earlier philosophers and theologians:

> The doctrines of those illustrious men, like the scattered members of a body, Thomas collected together and cemented, distributed in wonderful order, and so increased with important additions that he is rightly and deservedly esteemed the special bulwark and glory of the Catholic faith. With his spirit at once humble and swift, his memory ready and tenacious, his life spotless throughout, a lover of truth for its own sake, richly endowed with human and divine science, like the sun he heated the world with the warmth of his virtues and filled it with the splendor of his teaching.[6]

---

[6] Leo XIII, *Aeterni Patris*, §17.

THOMAS AQUINAS MAKES HISTORY

Another reason you should take St. Thomas seriously is that even people who aren't Catholic recognize the brilliance of his thought.

For example, if you take a philosophy 101 course in a public university, most of the philosophers you'll study will either be non-Christians (e.g., Socrates, David Hume) along with a few Christian lay people (e.g., Descartes, Kierkegaard), but almost every introductory philosophy text has a chapter dedicated to this medieval Dominican friar. They usually entrust Thomas with the classic arguments for the existence of God and acknowledge his role in giving them rigor and widespread appeal.

Aquinas' work on ethics and natural law has also had a profound impact on thinkers concerned with the role of justice and the State. Martin Luther King Jr. cited his thought in his "Letter from a Birmingham Jail," saying, "To put it in the terms of St. Thomas Aquinas: An unjust law is a human law that is not rooted in eternal law and natural law. Any law that uplifts human personality is just."[7]

However, not all philosophers believe St. Thomas is worthy of such admiration. Bertrand Russell said that Aquinas "is not engaged in an inquiry, the result of which it is impossible to know in advance. Before he begins to philosophize, he already knows the truth; it is declared in the Catholic faith. . . . The finding of arguments for a conclusion given in advance is not philosophy, but special pleading."[8]

---

[7] Martin Luther King Jr., "Letter from a Birmingham Jail," April 16, 1963. Available online at http://www.africa.upenn.edu/Articles_Gen/Letter_Birmingham.html.

[8] Bertrand Russell, *History of Western Philosophy* (New York: Simon and Schuster, 1945), 462.

But this is wrong on two counts.

First, all philosophers find arguments to support conclusions they accepted before engaging in philosophical inquiry. Philosophers who defend moral realism, for example, hold that moral truths like "torturing babies for fun is wrong" are true independent of human opinion (more than half of all professional philosophers, including non-religious ones, hold this view today). But I doubt these guys waited to believe torturing babies is always wrong until their sophomore year in college.

The philosopher Anthony Kenny (who wrote a criticism of Thomas' arguments for the existence of God) came to Aquinas' defense by pointing out, "It is extraordinary that that accusation should be made by Russell, who in the book *Principia Mathematica* takes hundreds of pages to prove that two and two make four, which is something he had believed all his life."[9]

Second, Thomas didn't just parrot what the Church had infallibly defined at earlier ecumenical councils. Instead he broached many "open questions" of theology and wasn't afraid to defend conclusions that he drew from the writings of Muslim and pagan philosophers. The bishops of Paris even condemned some of Aquinas' works in 1277 alongside the Muslim philosophers he quoted. But Aquinas was willing to risk being misunderstood by his peers in order to address the challenges posed by an Islamic school of thought called Averroeism.

Named after the twelfth-century Muslim philosopher Averroes, this school of Muslim philosophy claimed that reason was superior to faith and that the wisdom of the ancient Greek philosopher Aristotle should guide our reasoning. Aquinas agreed that Aristotle was a towering intellect (he even calls

---

[9]   Anthony Kenny, *Aquinas on Mind* (New York: Routledge, 1993), 12.

him "the Philosopher") but disagreed with the Averroeists and showed how faith and reason were complementary and could be used to examine one another.

That's why I absolutely hate when people go online and share this fake quote attributed to Aquinas: "To one who has faith, no explanation is necessary. To one without faith, no explanation is possible."[10] This makes no sense given that Aquinas wrote not just a book on explaining the faith to beginners who already believed in it (or the *Summa Theologiae*), but a book on explaining the faith to non-believers. It's called the *Summa Contra Gentiles*, and its full title in English is *Book on the truth of the Catholic faith against the errors of the unbelievers*.

THE WISDOM OF AQUINAS

Aquinas was intimately aware of the struggles that take place in our hearts and minds, and his work on psychology was actually revolutionary for his time. According to Eric L. Johnson, who is the co-editor of the book *Psychology and Christianity*, "[Aquinas] produced an influential body of psychological thought, covering the appetites, the will, habits, the virtues and vices, the emotions, memory, and the intellect."[11]

Here's one of his insights I really like: "Whatever is received into something is received according to the condition of the recipient."[12]

---

[10] For more on this quote, see Trent Horn, *What the Saints Never Said* (El Cajon, CA: Catholic Answers Press, 2018).

[11] Eric L. Johnson, "A History of Christians in Psychology," in *Psychology and Christianity*, eds. Eric L. Johnson and Stanton L. Jones (Downers Grove, IL: InterVarsity Press, 2000), 17.

[12] *Summa Theologiae* I, q. 75, a. 5. Hereafter cited as *ST*.

You've probably heard people describe teachers that go way over their student's heads as "trying to fill a paper cup with a fire hose." You can't get more than you're able to receive, be it intellectual truths or even spiritual gifts. The way that you receive a beautiful piece of music, for example, is going to be different to the way in which a seven-year-old receives it, because he's not mature enough. He hasn't experienced life enough. Perhaps his palate for the beautiful hasn't been refined as much as yours. Thomas especially understood this when it comes to pedagogy, or the art of teaching.

A student is not in the condition to receive advanced concepts unless he's mastered basic ones first. That's why Thomas criticized earlier works that appealed to scholars but frustrated beginners with "multiplication of useless questions, articles, and arguments" and "frequent repetition [which] brought weariness and confusion to the minds of readers." His works would be different because, as he says, "the doctor of Catholic truth ought not only to teach the proficient, but also to instruct beginners . . . we purpose in this book to treat of whatever belongs to the Christian religion, in such a way as may tend to the instruction of beginners."[13]

The *Summa Theologiae* is divided into three parts that deal with the major areas of Christian theology. In each part Aquinas deals with a variety of questions people struggle with, like, "Can the existence of God be proven?" What's fascinating about Thomas' approach here is that he always puts forth his opponent's best arguments. When you weaken an opponent's argument in order to make it easier to refute, that's called "straw-manning" because it's easier to beat up a scarecrow than a real person. The opposite is called "steel-manning," or

---

[13] *ST*, Prol.

taking your opponent's argument, making it better, and then still refuting it.

When you read Aquinas, you see that he is a master of steel-manning. Sometimes I read his description of objections to Christian theology and think, "Goodness, I'm not even sure how I'd respond to that. That sounds pretty convincing." But then he comes up with a reply that brings everything full circle, and he does so on a wide variety of topics.

The first part of the *Summa* has 119 questions, and they concern things like God's existence, God's nature, the creation of the world, angels, the nature of man. The second part has 303 questions. These concern things like morality in particular, including individual virtues and vices, and will be where we spend most of our time when it comes to the question, "What makes us truly happy?" Finally, the third part has about ninety questions concerning the person and the work of Jesus Christ in particular. But the third part is unfinished because on December 6, 1273, Thomas had a mystical experience that kept him from ever writing anything again.

When one of his religious brothers asked him why he had stopped writing, Thomas said in reply, "I can write no more. I have seen things that make my writings like straw."[14] Straw is what you put down for animals to, well, do their business on. Straw is what you throw into the stove to get the fire going. Thomas didn't think his work was worthless in and of itself (it's not like he ordered the *Summa* to be burned). But what he saw in this mystical experience was so good that his writings seemed infinitely inferior in comparison.

---

[14] Alban Butler, *Butler's Lives of the Saints*, eds. Herbert Thurston and Donald Attwater (Notre Dame, IN: Christian Classics, 1956), 511.

We don't know exactly what he saw, but one account says that after Mass Thomas would often rest his head on the tabernacle. One day, a fellow friar heard Christ speak to St. Thomas from the tabernacle. He said, "You've written well of me, Thomas. What shall be your reward?"

What did Thomas say?

If you're thinking of getting a tattoo or a new email signature, write this down: "Nothing if not you, Lord." Eleonore Stump, a philosopher who specializes in Thomistic thought, wrote, "He believed that he had at last clearly seen what he had devoted his life to figuring out and, by comparison, all he had written seemed pale and dry. Now that he could no longer write, he told Reginald, he wanted to die. Soon afterwards he did die, on 7 March 1274 at Fossanuova, Italy."[15]

---

[15] Eleonore Stump, *Aquinas* (New York: Routledge, 2003), 12.

3.

AQUINAS ON GOD AND HAPPINESS

WHEN YOU STUDY THE HISTORY OF "HAPPINESS," the weirdest thing you find is the newness of this concept. Don't misunderstand me: you can find cave drawings that show humans invented sports like wrestling and archery before they invented the wheel. But the constant threat of famine, war, and incurable diseases that brought about premature deaths and lifelong ailments always loomed in the background. The ancient Greek historian Herodotus said, "There is no human being either here or elsewhere so fortunate that it will not occur to him, often and not just once, to wish himself dead rather than alive."[1]

It's no wonder the seventeenth-century philosopher Thomas Hobbes called the lives people lived during that period of human existence "nasty, brutish, and short." But as civilization progressed and people could focus more on what they'd like to eat over how they would not like to be eaten, happiness became something that was more attainable but still outside of most people's grasp. If you were very rich or very

---

[1] Herodotus, *The Histories*, 7.46.3.

holy you might find happiness in this life, but once society became relatively Christianized, most people (especially the poor) accepted that sin would always result in suffering in this life, and so true happiness awaited the faithful who persevered until the end (see Matt 10:22).

However, as Darrin McMahon points out in his book *Happiness: A History*, after the industrial revolution people began to believe that happiness is something you could have in this life if you could afford it.

If you had enough money, you could have the right kind of food, medicine, and shelter that would protect you from harm and give you the freedom to pursue art, hobbies, and relationships that could make you happy. Happiness was now such a near possibility that in the modern age it has become a moral right: I have a right to be happy and nothing (even my spouse or children) can force me to do something that makes me unhappy. In 1643 John Milton wrote a tract criticizing the Church's laws that forbade divorce (which had been accepted since the time of Christ) because they turned marriage into "a drooping and disconsolate household captivity."

But even with all this stuff we can afford, and the freedom to do what we want, people seem to be less and less happy, especially in America. Alexis de Toqueville was a nineteenth-century French diplomat who wrote a wonderful commentary on American culture. In one part he says of Americans, "No one could work harder to be happy . . . [and yet] it seemed to me that a cloud habitually hung on their brow, and they seemed serious and almost sad even in their pleasures."[2]

---

[2] Darrin McMahon, *Happiness: A History* (New York: Grove/Atlantic, 2006), 334.

This would not have surprised Aquinas because he observed hundreds of years earlier that there are really two kinds of happiness and we become unhappy when we confuse them and try to find perfect happiness from an ultimately imperfect source.

PERFECT AND IMPERFECT HAPPINESS

In the *Summa Theologiae* Aquinas makes a distinction between perfect happiness (or what he calls *beatitude*) and imperfect happiness (or what he calls *felicitas*). Of the former kind of happiness Aquinas says:

> The object of the will, i.e. of man's appetite, is the universal good; just as the object of the intellect is the universal true. Hence it is evident that naught can lull man's will, save the universal good. This is to be found, not in any creature, but in God alone; because every creature has goodness by participation. Wherefore God alone can satisfy the will of man, according to the words of Psalm 102:5: "Who satisfieth thy desire with good things." Therefore God alone constitutes man's happiness.[3]

It would be easy for us to get caught up in this life and arguments for earthly goods leading to our highest happiness if we only had a finite amount of life ahead of us. But read almost any fictional treatment and you'll see the characters end up being horrified at lives that go on for centuries or millennia and become unbearably boring or pointless. That's why I think hell doesn't need little demons in red pajamas poking us in the rear end for all eternity; it just needs to be ourselves and any

---

[3] *ST* I-II, q. 2, a. 8.

finite earthly pleasure that will eventually become hellish after a few thousand years.

So there's nothing in this life that can give us the true happiness for which we were made. Aquinas says, "The goods of the present life pass away; since life itself passes away, which we naturally desire to have, and would wish to hold abidingly, for man naturally shrinks from death. Wherefore it is impossible to have true Happiness in this life."[4]

Is that it? Only God makes us happy and without God we're straight up out of luck? Not quite. Aquinas goes on to say, "Imperfect happiness that can be had in this life, can be acquired by man by his natural powers, in the same way as virtue, in whose operation it consists."[5]

We'll talk about how virtue and happiness are related in part three, but for now I want to focus on God himself, because if we don't really believe God exists and is the source of all goodness, then it can be really tempting to not want to follow the "straight and narrow" path he has set before us, even if we intellectually acknowledge God's existence.

C. S. Lewis wrote two amazing books on the problem of evil and suffering. The first was simply called *The Problem of Pain* and it was primarily a philosophical treatment of the problem. But the second one, *A Grief Observed*, was written after the death of his wife, which took a heavy toll on Lewis. He once said of the tragedies that befall people, "By our standards a mean joke; the monkey trick of a spiteful imbecile."[6]

---

4   *ST* I-II, q. 5, a. 3.
5   *ST* I-II, q. 5, a. 5.
6   C. S. Lewis. *A Grief Observed* (New York: HarperCollins Publishers, 1961), 18.

For a time, Lewis was angry with God, but he never gave up his faith because that wasn't an option. That would be like an orphan saying he never had biological parents because if he did they would have raised him. It makes sense for him to be angry at his parents' absence, but he can't just assume they never existed at all because if they didn't exist, then neither would he.

A similar logic helps me when I'm tempted to despair and think that God is the ultimate source, not of my happiness, but of my misery. I may not always understand why God has made happiness come from the difficult task of pursuing virtue, but I can't just say, "Never mind, I'm just going to become a hedonistic atheist," because atheism doesn't make sense to me. It doesn't make sense because of the reasons Aquinas gives to show that God exists.

So, with that said, let me share with you what I think is Aquinas' most powerful reason to believe that God exists: the argument from motion. What's great about it is that it doesn't assume we've proven from science that the universe began to exist and so God must have created it. Even if the universe were eternal (which Aquinas doesn't believe but grants for the sake of the argument), we would still arrive at the existence of God as the explanation for another curious fact about the universe: its propensity for change or motion.

GOD: THE ULTIMATE "ACTUALIZER"

When we look at the world around us, it becomes obvious that things change, which might be a more helpful word than Aquinas' use of "motion." Change is just what happens when potential becomes actual. My dog Lucy grew and died, thus making her potential future an actual past. We see objects change in size and a potential weight gain become an actual piling on of girth (like me when I forsake my paleo diet and just eat cake). Things change color. They change location. But how is it that things change?

Now, that might sound like a silly question, but it really isn't. The ancient Greek philosopher Parmenides thought change was an illusion because all that exists is being. Things either exist (being) or they don't exist (non-being). Now, if something were to change, that would be an example of something coming from nothing (being from non-being) or something disappearing into nothingness (being into non-being), both of which are impossible.

Take water, for example. It can be a liquid or a solid, but how is it able to go from liquid to solid? "Well, it freezes at a certain temperature, Matt! That's not hard to understand!" But that means water has the property of being solid and not solid at the same time, which seems like a contradiction in the same way a circle can't be "round" and "not round" at the same time.

So how do you resolve this apparent contradiction?

The only way, and it is Aristotle's genius that helps solve this issue, is to realize that things can exist either in *actuality* or in *potentiality*. So liquid water is actually wet and potentially solid. It can't be actually solid and not actually solid at the same time but it can be actually non-solid (i.e., liquid) and potentially solid (i.e., frozen when it gets cold) at the same time.

And here's the important part: its potential to become solid has to be activated by something else. Water can't freeze itself; something else has to act upon it in order to change it. And the potential in that force to freeze the water has to be actu-alized by something else. We then see that the entire universe is made up of chains of potentials being actualized by other things.

Now, here's the big question: Do these chains go backwards forever or do they terminate in an ultimate cause?

Another way to think about this that I find helpful is thinking about a train. Train cars on their own can't move themselves. And this is true no matter the length of the train. Even if you have an infinite series of train cars, it's going to stand perfectly still if it's composed of nothing but train cars.

For example, let's say you've got this big train called the Ghan that goes from Perth to Sydney. Sometimes you will come up to a railroad and you'll look left and right, and all you'll see is train because it appears like it's infinitely long. But of course you know that there has to be something other than train cars even though you don't see what it is that's moving it. You just know that there has to be, because train cars on their own can't move themselves.

In order to explain the motion of the train you need something that doesn't merely receive motion but actually gives motion without receiving it from anything else. In other words, you need a locomotive. Now, remember that change or motion is just the actualization of potential. But in order to explain why there is any change at all, the ultimate cause of the universe can't have anything potential about it. If it did, then its own motion or change would need to be explained by something else and then the process starts all over again. This ultimate cause must instead be pure actuality, or infinite being without any potentialities.

But is this cause God?

Well, it can't potentially "not exist" so it must be necessary and eternal. It can't potentially move or change so it can't be made of matter or exist within time. This cause is also the source of all change that moves from imperfect to more perfect. So all perfections, including changes in perfection like growth and knowledge and goodness, come from an all-knowing, all-good source of change. In other words, the motion and change in our universe can only be explained by an infinite, necessary, eternal, immaterial, all-powerful, all-knowing, all-good cause—or what most people call God.

So if all perfections ultimately come from a source of perfections, then it makes sense that we should strive for this source in our quest for happiness. But even people who know God is the source of all true happiness become distracted by the pleasures of this life. So, before we talk about how God truly makes us happy (and not in a cheap way like "Pray and it'll all be okay"), we need to talk about what *won't* make us truly happy. And that's the unpleasant subject we will turn to next.

SECTION 2

WHAT WILL *NOT* MAKE US HAPPY

4.

CAN SIN MAKE
ME HAPPY?

Even if you're not a religious person, you've probably heard of "The Seven Deadly Sins" (or saw the 1995 film *Seven* with Brad Pitt about a serial killer whose victims all allegedly commit these sins). However, these sins are more properly called the seven *capital* sins because the word "capital" comes from the word "head" and these sins are the source from which many other sins try to overtake our souls.

If you are a religious person, it should seem obvious that sin won't make us happy. But if that is true, then why do we keep on sinning? St. John even says, "If we say we have no sin, we deceive ourselves, and the truth is not in us" (1 John 1:8). So, in order to be happy we have to confront the reason why we so often turn to sin to give us the happiness we know only comes from God alone.

Before I tell you what these seven capital sins are, you should know I'll be referencing a work by Pope St. Gregory the Great called *The Books of the Morals: an exposition on the book of Blessed Job*. This is the source that Aquinas uses in the *Summa*, especially when he addresses the issues of vice and virtue, so if it's good enough for him, then it's good enough for me!

Here's an easy way to remember these sins that I learned from the Catholic philosopher Taylor Marshall. It's an acronym: PALE GAS.

I don't know what you think of when you think of PALE GAS but it sounds nasty enough to represent the seven deadly sins. With that acronym in mind, here they are: **P**ride, **A**nger, **L**ust, **E**nvy, **G**luttony, **A**varice, and **S**loth.

PRIDE

Pride is easily the most dangerous of all the capital sins. Aquinas says, "The first sin of the angel can be none other than pride" and the fall of the angels is attributed to their desire "not to be subject to a superior when subjection is due." Adam and Eve, like the angels, sinned by desiring a spiritual good beyond their authority to possess it—to be like God in a way of their choosing. Because of this, as Aquinas says, "it follows that man's first sin consisted in his coveting some spiritual good above his measure: and this pertains to pride. Therefore it is evident that man's first sin was pride."[1]

When's the last time you confessed the sin of pride?

I don't know about you, but sometimes, I'll be standing in line for confession, and I'll think to myself, "Well, I don't think I did anything huge this time around, so what can I say so at least it looks like I'm thinking properly about sin?" which is probably in itself the sin of pride. Or at least it leads to what pride really is: an excessive esteem about one's own excellence.

---

[1] *ST* II-II, q. 163, q. 1.

Pride is often manifested in things like vanity, narcissism, and being overly concerned with our appearance, intelligence, or status. We often don't think we've committed the sin of pride because we confuse it with self-love. Jesus said we ought to love our neighbor as we love ourself, so that means we should love and esteem ourselves, right?

Not so fast.

The fourteenth-century poet Dante Alighieri described pride as a love of self that is perverted to hatred and contempt for one's neighbor. Pride craves the approval of others and seeks our good above the good of others. "Self-love" consumes the good of love so much that only the "self" with its inexhaustible desires remains.

Do we really want to live this way? If you don't, then the antidote to pride is humility, which, as Aquinas says, "expels pride" and "makes man submissive and ever open to receive the influx of Divine grace. Hence it is written (James 4:6): 'God resisteth the proud, and giveth grace to the humble.'"[2]

One way to grow in humility is to pray Rafael Cardinal Merry del Val's Litany of Humility, which ends with a sentiment that will truly bring us the happiness that pride can never deliver. We hope "that others may be preferred to me in everything. That others may become holier than I, provided that I may become as holy as I should: Jesus, grant me the grace to desire it."

ANGER

Aquinas tells us that, "inasmuch as the movement of the sen-

---

[2] *ST* II-II, q. 161, a. 5.

sitive appetite is directed against vice and in accordance with reason, this anger is good, and is called 'zealous anger.'"[3] This corresponds to St. Paul's advice to "be angry but do not sin; do not let the sun go down on your anger" (Eph 4:26).

So if you get mad about an abusive parent you heard about on the news, you're not engaged in the sin of anger; you're being a completely normal human being. Anger is our reaction to an injustice in the world; it is the fuel for the engine that seeks to destroy evils and rebuild goods that have been lost. But we have to be careful, because Aquinas says:

> On the other hand, if one desire the taking of vengeance in any way whatever contrary to the order of reason, for instance if he desire the punishment of one who has not deserved it, or beyond his deserts, or again contrary to the order prescribed by law, or not for the due end, namely the maintaining of justice and the correction of defaults, then the desire of anger will be sinful, and this is called sinful anger.[4]

So when do we feel anger overwhelming us? Usually it's when we think someone is going to cause harm to ourselves or a loved one and our first instinct is to harm them, to balance the scales of justice, if you will. Somebody says something on your Twitter feed that's a little nasty. You don't just want to reply in kind. You really want to drive the dagger in and twist it.

So what's the answer to sinful anger? Gratitude. We get angry when we feel like we weren't given what we deserve, be it time, money, or even respect. Gratitude helps us to be grateful for

---

3   *ST* II-II, q. 158, a. 1.

4   *ST* II-II, q. 158, a. 2.

what we actually have and stop worrying about what we didn't get at any given moment. Aquinas says:

> Since true friendship is based on virtue, whatever there is contrary to virtue in a friend is an obstacle to friendship, and whatever in him is virtuous is an incentive to friendship. In this way friendship is preserved by repayment of favors, although repayment of favors belongs specially to the virtue of gratitude.[5]

LUST

St. Gregory says the sin of lust whispers in our ears that if God didn't want us to engage in sexual intercourse whenever it strikes our fancy, "he would not at the first beginning of the human race have made them male and female."[6]

Isn't this the same lie we tell ourselves? We say, "If God didn't want me looking at porn, masturbating, hooking up with people, going to a massage parlor, seeking out a prostitute—then he wouldn't have given me sexual desires for these things. Why has God given me all these sexual desires if he's asking me to say no to all of them?"

Of course, the answer to lustful desires is not to give into them; that's like drinking seawater to satiate thirst. The answer is chastity, which isn't a naïve rejection of our sexuality that tells us to repress all our sexual feelings, put our fingers in our ears, and shout, "La La La, I can't hear you, lustful thoughts." It is instead a mastery of our sexuality and ordering it to our good

---

[5] *ST* II-II, q. 106, a. 1.

[6] St. Gregory, *Moralia in Job*, §90. Available online at http://www.lectionarycentral.com/trinity03/Gregorymoralia2.html.

and the good of others. Aquinas even gives us four practical ways to overcome lust and achieve this kind of mastery.

The first is to avoid those occasions of sin that overwhelm us. He advises, in the words of Sirach 9:5–9, "Gaze not upon a maiden lest her beauty be a stumbling-block to thee. . . . Look not around about thee in the ways of the city, nor wander up and down in the streets thereof." If he were alive today, St. Thomas might say something like, "Disconnect from the Internet, or at least get accountability or filtering software to monitor your web browsing."

The second and third way is to not give "an opening to thoughts which of themselves are the occasion of lustful desires." We can do this by training our bodies not to rely on bodily pleasures for "quick hits" of happiness (a technique called "mortification"), and by strengthening ourselves through prayer. Or, as Thomas puts it,

> All this is not unlike to a fight between two persons, one of whom you desire to win, the other to lose. You must sustain the one and withdraw all support from the other. So also between the spirit and the flesh there is a continual combat. Now, if you wish the spirit to win, you must assist it by prayer, and likewise you must resist the flesh by such means as fasting; for by fasting the flesh is weakened.

Finally, stay busy in good things so that the mind does not have time to entertain impure thoughts. Aquinas quotes Jerome in this regard, who says, "Be always busy in doing something good, so that the devil may find you ever occupied."[7]

---

[7] St. Thomas Aquinas, "Explanation of the Ten Commandments."

ENVY

St. Gregory says envy "is also wont to exhort the conquered heart" by whispering seductive questions to us like, "In what art thou inferior to this or that person? Why then art thou not either equal or superior to them? What greater things art thou able to do, which they are not able to do! They ought not then to be either superior, or even equal to thyself."[8]

Envy is related to pride because our desire to be esteemed by others can only seem to be satisfied if we have that which *we esteem in them*. And if we can't have that, we end up hating our neighbor for being better than us. Envy brings with it, as Gregory tells us, "hatred, whispering, detraction, exultation at the misfortunes of a neighbor, and affliction at his prosperity." For many of us, this takes place once we're safely out of earshot of our neighbor.

Envy is when I'm on Instagram and I see families posting photos about their perfect little life and their car and their perfectly neat house and their vacations and all these things and it makes me sick. That's why Aquinas describes envy as "sorrow at another's good." But instead of being sorrowful, we should rejoice. And there lies the key to overcoming envy: kindness and rejoicing in others' fortune. Aquinas says that

> it behooves man to be maintained in a becoming order towards other men as regards their mutual relations with one another, in point of both deeds and words, so that they behave towards one another in a becoming manner. Hence the need of a special virtue

Available online at https://www.ewtn.com/catholicism/library/explanation-of-the-ten-commandments--1452.

[8] St. Gregory, *Moralia in Job*, §90.

that maintains the becomingness of this order: and this virtue is called friendliness.[9]

So, when you're tempted to be envious of what other people have, take a moment to be a friend to those people (even if they don't know you) and thank God for how he blessed them. It's hard to do at first, but over time it becomes second nature and feels way better than just griping about somebody else's life.

GLUTTONY

My parents always said, "Don't drink out of the cereal bowl." Don't worry, I'm not saying that you're a bad parent or a bad person if you do drink out of the cereal bowl. But I think there's a good point to it. They might also say, "Don't eat like a pig." And what they mean by that is something rather theologically precise.

There are five ways St. Thomas Aquinas says that we can commit the sin of gluttony: we might desire food and drink too soon, too expensively, too much, too eagerly, or too daintily. According to Fr. Dwight Longenecker,

> Gluttony includes any form of addiction. Drug abuse, caffeine or sugar addictions and alcoholism are forms of gluttony, but so is any inordinate attachment to food and drink. . . . A person who insists on their steak being done "just so" then complains and rejects it is also placing too much selfish attention on food.[10]

---

[9] *ST* II-II, q. 114, a. 1.

[10] Fr. Dwight Longenecker, "Seeking Satisfaction—Gluttony," *Catholic Exchange,* September 24, 2014. Available online at https://catholicexchange.com/seeking-satisfaction-gluttony.

Doesn't it always happen that we think to ourselves, "Gosh, I should have just stopped with that one"? It's like when you get this dessert, and you eat it, and it's absolutely mind blowing. Then you innocently say, "I'll have one more" because you want to recreate the same experience you had when you first ate it. But when you do, it's not as good as the first time.

The sin of gluttony arises when we incessantly chase happiness through food and drink, when these earthly things displace our proper end in God. They also weaken our resolve against sin, or as Gregory puts it, "When the belly is distended by gluttony, the virtues of the soul are destroyed by lust." St. Paul likewise said, "Their end is destruction, their god is the belly, and they glory in their shame, with minds set on earthly things. But our commonwealth is in heaven, and from it we await a Savior, the Lord Jesus Christ" (Phil 3:19–20).

But our bodies and souls are strengthened by the virtue of temperance, which keeps things in their proper balance. It's like the keel that keeps the ship of our souls from capsizing or the base of one of those toy "inflatable referees" that causes him to always pop up no matter how hard you hit him. That's why Aquinas says that "the end and rule of temperance itself is happiness; while the end and rule of the thing it makes use of is the need of human life, to which whatever is useful for life is subordinate."[11]

AVARICE

There's always a way you can make money. You might not make a lot of money, but hey, you can start a blog, sell T-shirts, start

---

[11] *ST* II-II, q. 141, a. 6.

a podcast, maybe call it *Pints With Aquinas*, and have a Patreon account. There are all sorts of ways we can make money, and because of that, we can kind of fall into a trap of always being concerned with needing more money.

Why? Why do you need more? Sometimes this is the result of not trusting in God to meet our needs. But just as food can't bring enduring peace to our bodies, money can't bring a similar kind of peace to our souls. As we've seen, while the Bible does not condemn money in and of itself, it does consider money an easy source of temptation. That's why one of the wise men quoted in the book of Proverbs simply prays, "give me neither poverty nor riches; feed me with the food that is needful for me" (30:8).

So what's the antidote to being consumed with avarice and being a slave to money? Generosity. St. Thomas Aquinas says that giving away money, in a sense, makes us stronger by building up that "moral muscle memory." He writes that "in parting with a thing—for instance, when we throw something—the farther we put it away the greater the force [*virtus*] employed. Hence parting with money by giving it to others proceeds from a greater virtue than when we spend it on ourselves."

I know from my own life that I sometimes regret spending money on myself because I end up still being unsatisfied but with a thinner wallet. But I never regret giving away money to those who are genuinely in need. So if you feel like money has made you a slave, consider giving away a small amount you know you could survive without, like $5 a month. Then, make a budget to track your expenses so that money doesn't just "disappear" each month. As you get better at tracking money, you'll find that you can devote more income to paying down debt and then, once your debts are paid off, you can focus on using extra money to help others.

Obviously there is a whole lot more that could be said about the "how-to" of financial health, but the main point is this: money isn't what solves our problems. We solve our problems by using our God-given wisdom to direct what we've been blessed with (including money) towards achieving good in the world. And when we do that, we stop seeking the fleeting pleasure of having *things* and experience the abiding joy of having *God* animate our very being and move us to do his will.

SLOTH

This one's not a creepy little bugger who hangs out in trees (but his slow behavior does give us a clue about this sin). Gregory calls this sin "melancholy," saying it will "exhort the conquered heart as if with reason when it says, 'What ground hast thou to rejoice when thou endures so many wrongs from thy neighbor?'" Fr. John Hardon defines it as "sluggishness of soul or boredom because of the exertion necessary for the performance of a good work. The good work may be a corporal task, such as walking; or a mental exercise, such as writing; or a spiritual duty, such as prayer."[12]

Sloth is a sin, not in the sense of an overt action or desire like anger and greed, but in the absence of good desires and actions. It's an absence manifested by sadness and dejection in the face of God's good gifts, so it represents ingratitude towards him.

We usually feel sloth after being overwhelmed by life. We can

---

[12] John A. Hardon, *Modern Catholic Dictionary* (New York: Image, 2013), electronic edition.

get to the point where we don't make a conscious decision to be slothful but it ends up happening anyway. It might be something as simple as dwelling on this thought: "What's the point of getting excited about life when all this bad stuff keeps happening to me? I may as well live with massively low expectations and at least that way I won't be disappointed."

I went to confession recently, and one of the things I confessed was this lack of joy that I sometimes have when I'm with my family and when I'm with my kids. I'm always nitpicking, I'm always worried about them spilling milk on the counter or dropping food on the ground. I wish I could relax and think to myself, "It's just food. I'll clean it up later because the kids are having fun." When I confessed this the priest said to me, "It's very important that the father of the house be joyful."

And therein lies the antidote to sloth: finding joy in the work we are called to do. It may not be glamorous work. People may fail to thank us for it, but when we know that we are giving God our best in the tasks he has assigned to us on earth, then that removes the temptation to despair at the burdens we have to carry in this life.

EXPELLING PALE GAS

These seven deadly sins will make us lose our reason, and, if we do not repent of them, will lead us to eternal damnation. Let's repent of them. The best way to do that is to make a good confession and to do that we need to make a good examination of conscience. Here's a quick way to do it. As you're lying in bed, think of those things, PALE GAS. You can also divide it up, as the PALE sins deal with sins involving other *people*, whereas the GAS sins deal with sins involving other *things*.

Ask yourself: How have I **pridefully** elevated myself over God and other people? How have I been **angry** in a way that merely seeks injury to people who have wronged me? How have I **lusted** after people who are not my beloved spouse? How have I been **envious** of the goods that others have?

Envy is sort of the bridge into the GAS sins because the objects we sinfully desire are the goods, talents, and blessings that belong to other people. But when it comes to things that we think will make us happy, we should ask ourselves: How have I treated food, drink, or substances in a **gluttonous** way? How have I practiced **avarice**, or greed, when it comes to things like hoarding money? And finally, how have I been **slothful**? How have I turned inward away from other people, things, and even God, and felt like I shouldn't even try to be holy?

But don't let an honest self-inventory become an unanswerable accuser that perpetually keeps you away from God.

When I was at World Youth Day in Toronto in the year 2002, Pope St. John Paul II said to us, "We are not the sum of our weaknesses and failures; we are the sum of the Father's love for us and our real capacity to become the image of his Son." The same thing is true of you, too. No matter how immersed in sin you are, no matter how hopeless it may seem, with God's grace you can begin to become the person he wants you to be, fully alive (see John 10:10)!

5.

CAN BODILY PLEASURES MAKE ME HAPPY?

IT WAS ABOUT 9 P.M. and my wife and I had finally gotten the kids down after a very long and trying day. I was rummaging through the pantry when my wife asked, "What are you looking for?"

"Happiness," I responded.

A pretty honest moment, I thought. I was looking for something to give me peace and satisfaction. And I know I'm not alone. All of us can fall into this trap in one way or another.

We feel stressed, exhausted, or agitated, and we reach to something outside ourselves: food, drink, sex, entertainment, etc., to make us happy. And while these external goods are blessings the Lord may want for us, they aren't our ultimate good and therefore cannot ultimately satisfy us.

CAN MONEY MAKE US HAPPY?

Aquinas may confidently say that wealth can't make us happy, but I don't think most of us are as confident as him. If you came up to me and said, "Here's $100,000," that would make me *really* happy—or at least it would make me really excited. But Aquinas gives us an argument to show why money can't give us true happiness. First, he makes a distinction between two kinds of wealth, natural and artificial:

> Natural wealth is that which serves man as a remedy for his natural wants: such as food, drink, clothing, cars, dwellings, and such like, while artificial wealth is that which is not a direct help to nature, as money, but is invented by the art of man, for the convenience of exchange, and as a measure of things salable.[1]

The difference between natural wealth and artificial wealth is like the difference between a pizza and a gift card to the local pizzeria. If you were stuck on a desert island, you'd want the pizza since you can't eat a gift card. But, in most cases, if I offered you a "free pizza," you'd probably want the gift card so you could eat the pizza at your convenience. The pizza is a piece of natural wealth that can satisfy your desires, whereas the gift card, or any kind of money, is a piece of artificial wealth that you can trade for that which can immediately satisfy your desires. Aquinas continues:

> Now it is evident that man's happiness cannot consist in natural wealth. For wealth of this kind is sought for the sake of something else, viz. as a support of human nature: consequently it cannot be man's last end, rather is it ordained to man as to its end. Wherefore in the order of nature, all such things are below man, and made for him, according to Psalm 8:8: "Thou hast

---

[1] *ST* I-II, q. 2. a. 1.

subjected all things under his feet."[2]

Natural wealth can't make us happy because we don't seek these things for themselves. We seek these things to help us survive. They are not the ultimate ends we seek but a means to those ends. We all know this. You've never bought something and then said to yourself, "I am completely happy!" We thought that would work when we were five and six, and then after we got the thing, we just started looking to the next thing and, of course, we still do that today.

Indeed, some of the best evidence for Aquinas' argument comes from the lives of people like lottery winners or celebrities who have attained massive amounts of wealth. If money makes people happy, they should be dancing in the streets. They should be completely joyful people who sleep well at night and who don't need to go to narcotics or prostitutes for thrills, because they should be happy. They shouldn't be committing suicide. In fact, a study from the Federal Reserve showed suicide rates are higher in wealthier neighborhoods, possibly because people are under constant pressure to not just be wealthy but keep up with their wealthier neighbors in an endless pursuit of material prosperity.[3]

CAN STUFF MAKE US HAPPY?

Aquinas says that when we obtain God, or as we grow in relationship with him, we love him more and more. And this isn't

---

[2] *ST* I-II, q. 2, a. 1.

[3] Josh Sanburn, "Why Suicides Are More Common in Richer Neighborhoods," *Time Magazine*, November 8, 2012. Available online at http://business.time.com/2012/11/08/why-suicides-are-more-common-in-richer-neighborhoods/.

just true of God; this is true of those we begin to love in this life. When I first got married, I felt "in love" with my wife and couldn't imagine being even more in love but now that I've been married fifteen years, I want to say to her, "You are way better than I thought you were when we got married, and back then I thought you were the best!"

But when it comes to artificial things, we don't grow in that same love. Instead, we end up despising those things and we want something else to replace them. That's why Aquinas says, "Hence it is written (Sirach 24:29): 'They that eat me shall yet hunger,'... which is the sense of Our Lord's words (John 4:13): 'Whosoever drinketh of this water,' by which temporal goods are signified, 'shall thirst again.'"[4]

It wasn't until I read the *Summa Theologiae* that I thought about the water our blessed Lord speaks of as signifying temporal goods, but it's a wonderful point. Christ says to the woman who has come to draw water at the well in John 4:13, "Every one who drinks of this water will thirst again."

What's the latest thing you really wanted? I mean *really* wanted?

One example for myself was a wooden churchwarden tobacco pipe like the one Gandalf smokes in *The Lord of the Rings*. I actually won it in a bet and was really excited to get it. Now, to be fair, I didn't place all my happiness in it, but I was really excited to get it.

And then when I got it, the most exciting thing was opening the box. Judging by the tens of millions of people who watch online videos that only consist of toys and trinkets being unwrapped, a

---

[4] *ST* I-II, q. 2, a. 1.

lot of people feel the same way. But after you unwrap it, you feel like saying, "Okay. That's good. Now what?"

We get really excited about obtaining these things, and then, as Aquinas says, we end up despising them. And he says the reason for this is that "we realize more their insufficiency when we possess them." When we're incapable of possessing things, we can mistakenly believe that, if we had them, they would make us happy (be it a thing or even a person with whom we are infatuated). But when we obtain them, we realize that they can't fill the void in our hearts that is the root cause of our unhappiness.

In fact, there's a whole movement of people who understand this and try to live a life of minimalism. They know that as we accumulate more stuff, we accumulate more worry about our stuff. We worry about it breaking, being stolen, or eventually fading in quality over time. We worry that other people won't be impressed by our stuff or that we need newer stuff to make us happy because the old stuff is now inferior or obsolete in comparison.

There's a classic study that I love to share with people who become obsessed with things making them happy. Researchers asked two groups of people about their current levels of happiness: people who had just won the lottery and people who had just been confined to wheelchairs because of an accident. They specifically asked them about how everyday interactions, like eating lunch or talking with friends, made them happy. It turns out that the lottery winners averaged 3.33 out of 5 when it comes to daily happiness, whereas the accident victims averaged 3.48 out of 5. Here's how the authors of the study explain the lack of increased happiness among the lottery winners:

Eventually, the thrill of winning the lottery will itself wear off. If all things are judged by the extent to which they depart from a baseline of past experience, gradually even the most positive events will cease to have impact as they themselves are absorbed into the new baseline against which further events are judged. Thus, as lottery winners become accustomed to the additional pleasures made possible by their new wealth, these pleasures should be experienced as less intense and should no longer contribute very much to their general level of happiness.[5]

Ecclesiastes 5:10 says, "He who loves money will not be satisfied with money; nor he who loves wealth with gain: this also is vanity."

Here's a suggestion for you and me if we really want to take this to prayer. Imagine the kind of number that you think would suffice to make you secure, to make you feel secure and in control, and be as audacious as you like. Some of you might say $50,000. Others might say, "Hmm, one million. If I had one million dollars, then I could do what I want." And all of us would say something like, "No, I wouldn't be irresponsible. I'd donate some of it to charity or my church, but then I could just get on with the business of life."

Put yourself in that position, and then imagine that you're told by your doctor that you're dying of some disease. At that point, nothing matters. None of that money matters to us at least. We might think about the good we can do with it, but as far as the security and control we thought it could buy us, it

---

5   Philip Brickman, Dan Coates, and Ronnie Janoff-Bulman, "Lottery Winners and Accident Victims: Is Happiness Relative?" *Journal of Personality and Social Psychology* 36, no. 8 (1978): 918.

can't. Jesus made the same point in a parable about a wealthy man who hoarded his money. God said to the man "'Fool! This night your soul is required of you; and the things you have prepared, whose will they be?' So is he who lays up treasure for himself, and is not rich toward God" (Luke 12:20–21).

Don't get confused, however, in all this talk about money not making us happy, to think this means money is evil. In 1 Timothy 6:10 St. Paul says, "For the love of money is the root of all evils; it is through this craving that some have wandered away from the faith and pierced their hearts with many pangs."

Paul doesn't say *money* is the root of all evil. He says, "For the *love* of money is a root of all kinds of evil" (ESV). St. Thomas Aquinas defines sin as the result of loving creatures more than creator. Money (or *anything*) becomes evil when we love it more than God, which is a problem that ends up accompanying the other earthly pleasures in our brief survey.

WHEN PLEASURE BECOMES ADDICTION

Another reason we should reject pleasure as the source of our happiness is that, along with being unable to provide us with true happiness, this pursuit of pleasure can easily lead to the unhappy entrapment of addiction. While drugs and even some kinds of food can be very addictive, one of the most destructive forms of addiction I've fought and helped others to fight is addiction to sexual pleasure: particularly to the pleasure that comes from viewing pornography.

What would Aquinas say to those of us who think that sexual pleasure is necessary for our happiness?

First, Aquinas was not a prude who believed sex was an evil

result of original sin that we had to put up with in order to have babies. In his article "Thomas Aquinas on Sexual Pleasure," John Giles Milhaven says that Aquinas "rejects the widespread medieval position that this appetite (*concupiscentia*) is essentially sinful. He also denies—and is the first medieval theologian to do so—that this appetite constitutes a flaw or perversion of human nature."[6]

Aquinas did not believe that sexual pleasure should be sought as an end in itself, as if the spouse were just a pleasure dispenser. But he also did not condemn the pleasure that naturally flows from the sexual act. Aquinas even wrote of "the greatest bodily pleasure which is that of sexual intercourse" as being the reason why voluntarily abstaining from sexual relations can be such a profound virtue.[7] Instead, he points out that

> it belong[s] to the perfection of moral good, that man should be moved unto good, not only in respect of his will, but also in respect of his sensitive appetite; according to Psalm 83:3: "My heart and my flesh have rejoiced in the living God": where by "heart" we are to understand the intellectual appetite, and by "flesh" the sensitive appetite.[8]

Just as it is licit to seek a union with God that includes our body as well as our soul, we can seek a complete "one-flesh union" with our spouse. A 2019 study confirms that religious couples that attend weekly church services have the most satisfying sex lives.[9] But this does not mean that people who

---

[6] John Giles Milhaven, "Thomas Aquinas on Sexual Pleasure," *The Journal of Religious Ethics* 5, no. 2 (Fall 1977): 159.

[7] *ST* II-II, q. 152, a. 1.

[8] *ST* I-II, q. 24, a. 3.

[9] David French, "The Sexual Revolutionaries Got Sexual Satisfaction

choose to live an unmarried life (like priests and religious) or people who desire marriage but are unable to find a spouse are doomed to an unhappy life.

Finally, if you're struggling with sexual sin, know that you're not alone, you're not a freak, and that help is available to you.

Sometimes people fall into the trap of thinking that marriage will cure lust, but if that were true, then why do married people—even married people who have sex regularly—struggle with porn and other sexual sins? The truth is that marriage won't cure us of our lust, but our lust may just destroy our marriage. Whether you're married or single, don't be so prideful as to try and fight this alone. Reach out and find help. One place you might go is to strive21.com, which hosts a series of courses I helped create for people who want to break free of sexual sin.

CAN EARTHLY PLEASURES MAKE US TRULY HAPPY?

Hedonism is the belief that happiness ultimately comes from pleasure, or that I will be happy when I feel good. "If I just had the right food, television shows, and person to experience sexual intimacy with, then I'd be happy!"

Now, there is an intuitive connection between pleasure and happiness in that they are both ends in themselves. In other words, you might ask someone why he goes to school or work but not why he wants to be happy or experience pleasure. The

All Wrong," *National Review,* May 22, 2019. Available online at https://www.nationalreview.com/2019/05/the-sexual-revolution-aries-got-sexual-satisfaction-all-wrong/.

person just does, which means pleasure must be good in itself if not the ultimate source of our happiness. But just because two things share a common feature does not mean they are the same thing.

Dolphins and humans are both warm-blooded but you won't see me jumping through rings at SeaWorld for fish anytime soon (well, unless the sales of this book go poorly). No, pleasure and happiness are distinct, and while pleasure is something we experience when we are happy, pleasure in itself is not the source of happiness. Rather, like we saw with sin, seeking bodily pleasures as the ultimate source of our happiness is a shortcut that never really satisfies us.

To show that bodily pleasures are not the ultimate source of our happiness, Aquinas quotes the early medieval philosopher Boethius, who also wrestled with the question of happiness in his book, *The Consolation of Philosophy.* He said something that most people who have had too much to drink can easily relate to: "Any one that chooses to look back on his past excesses, will perceive that pleasures had a sad ending: and if they can render a man happy, there is no reason why we should not say that the very beasts are happy too."[10]

If pleasure alone makes us happy, then animals should be just as happy as us. Or, to put it another way, once we have had all our pleasures satiated, we should be just as content as our pets. But you probably don't come home to the sight of your dog forlornly looking out the window as if to say, "What's the point of all this?" At best, they are just bored as they wait for another "pleasure hit" that comes from playing with their owner.

---

[10] *ST* I-II, q. 2, a. 6.

That works for finite, material beings like pets, but not for human beings. Aquinas notes that "since the rational soul excels the capacity of corporeal matter, that part of the soul which is independent of a corporeal organ, has a certain infinity in regard to the body and those parts of the soul which are tied down to the body."[11]

In other words, we have a natural desire for happiness that is unending in quantity and unsurpassed in quality.

The philosopher Robert Nozick offers a thought experiment that shows why pleasure is not our ultimate good, even if it could be unending in duration. Nozick asks if you would want to be hooked up to a virtual reality "pleasure machine" akin to the false reality of the Matrix films. In this world you could have anything you wanted, any way you wanted. But most people would not want to have pleasure that is derived from illusory people and things.

We desire goods that come from interactions with real people and things—or goods that actualize our full potential as human beings made in the image and likeness of God.

---

[11] *ST* I-II, q. 2, a. 6.

6.

CAN INTERIOR PLEASURES MAKE ME HAPPY?

I ONCE TOOK MY FAMILY TO NEW ZEALAND and we went to Hobbiton, the site where Peter Jackson filmed the Shire for *The Lord of the Rings*. When we arrived, we hopped on the bus with twenty or so tourists and were greeted by our tour guide. When she came up to us, she stopped in her tracks and asked me if I was Matt Fradd.

I was taken aback before saying that, yes, I was. She told me that it was in large part because of my podcast, *Pints With Aquinas*, that she ended up coming back to the Catholic Church. I was stunned and grateful to God. And, if I'm honest, I was totally tempted towards being filled with pride. I'm still tempted to that (which, let's be honest, is probably at least part of why I'm sharing the story in this book). All of us in some way or another will be tempted to think that power and influence are what will make us happy. But at the end of the day, they won't. They can't. And Aquinas shows us why.

CAN POWER MAKE US HAPPY?

In *The Prince*, Machiavelli said, "It is better to be feared than loved, if you cannot be both." Some people find happiness in the power they have over other people. Maybe they're the boss who always get praise from subordinates or even a parent who loves being the "king" or "queen" of the castle. But Aquinas says, "Happiness is the perfect good. But power is most imperfect." He then quotes Boethius, who asks, "Think you a man is powerful who is surrounded by attendants, whom he inspires with fear indeed, but whom he fears still more?"[1]

No one can truly be happy from his power over others because that power is always tenuous. Think of Julius Caesar, who basically had the whole world in the palm of his hand until he was stabbed in the back by the people over whom he supposedly had power. Power can't make us happy because only a good can make us happy, and power is just a means to a good.

At the most basic level, power is the ability to do something. You have a rational power because you can read this book, unless this is an audiobook. But even then, you have the power to hear and understand what I'm saying. Aquinas says that "some happiness might consist in the good use of power, which is by virtue, rather than in power itself."

I love one of the objections that Aquinas answers in relation to his claim that power does not lead to happiness: "It would seem that happiness consists in power. For all things desire to become like to God, as to their last end and first beginning. But men who are in power, seem, on account of the similarity of power, to be most like to God."

---

[1]   *ST* I-II, q. 2, a. 4.

At first, that seems right. If we're like God, we will be happy. God is all-powerful, so the more power we have, the happier we will be.

In reply, Aquinas points out that in God there is no difference between his goodness and his power. God is infinite being itself, and we have to make distinguishing categories in our minds in order to understand him. But God is solely one perfect, simple act of being, or perfection. So there is no way God can misuse his power for evil because he is, by definition, good. The *Catechism* says, "God's almighty power is in no way arbitrary," and then quotes Aquinas, who wrote in the *Summa*, "In God, power, essence, will, intellect, wisdom, and justice are all identical. Nothing therefore can be in God's power which could not be in his just will or his wise intellect" (271).

We are fallen creatures, and because of this we need checks and balances to keep us from using our power to abuse others. That's why Lord Acton famously said, "Power tends to corrupt and absolute power corrupts absolutely." The only being that can handle absolute power is that being who is also absolute goodness by necessity, or God.

But maybe the problem with trying to derive happiness from power is that we try to use power as a means to get other people to respect us. If they loved something about us rather than the power we have over them, then wouldn't that make us happy?

CAN HONOR MAKE US HAPPY?

Okay, so maybe stuff or things outside of us can't make us happy. But maybe people outside of us can make us happy if they praise us and think we're awesome. At least, as you've seen, I've felt that temptation on occasions. However, Aquinas says that neither fame nor honor can make us happy. When it comes to honor, he says:

> It is impossible for happiness to consist in honor. For honor is given to a man on account of some excellence in him; and consequently it is a sign and attestation of the excellence that is in the person honored. . . . As the Philosopher says (Ethic. i, 5), honor is not that reward of virtue, for which the virtuous work: but they receive honor from men by way of reward, "as from those who have nothing greater to offer." But virtue's true reward is happiness itself, for which the virtuous work: whereas if they worked for honor it would no longer be a virtue, but ambition.[2]

Alright, let's break this down. We want honor, or praise, or fame, or whatever you want to call it. We think that having honor will make us happy but it can't do that because honor isn't in *us*, it's in the person who's honoring us and happiness has to be within us in order to make us truly happy.

If you were on a desert island and caught a juicy fish, you could have the pleasure of eating that food or feel confident in your accomplishment, but you couldn't have honor because no one's around to give it to you. Here is a case where you could have happiness without any honors associated with it. Since happiness exists within you, honor can't be that which makes us truly happy.

The other point Aquinas makes is that honor can't make us happy because it's a sign of some other good thing that makes us happy. If we just had the honor without the good quality

---

[2] *ST* I-II, q. 2, a. 2.

associated with it, we wouldn't really be happy. For example, have you ever played in kids' sports and gotten a participation trophy? It's great to get a trophy, but as an adult it would be sad if you showed off participation trophies to friends, because you didn't do anything to earn them. You just showed up.

Or consider this example: would you rather be honored for doing something evil or vilified for doing something good?

In 1931 August Landmesser joined the Nazi party in Germany because he thought it was the only way to get a decent job. However, four years later he was expelled from the party for being engaged to a Jewish woman named Irma Eckler. A year later, in 1936, Landmesser was at the Blohm+Voss shipyard in Hamburg where a Nazi rally was taking place and a picture was taken of everyone in the crowd giving the Nazi salute—except for Landmesser.

It's a famous photograph and I hope you'll look it up because you should ask yourself: Would I have the guts to stand up to evil even if it meant not just dishonor, but death? Landmesser and Eckler chose to do so, and Eckler paid for that choice with her life at the Ravensbrück concentration camp in 1942.

Don't you wish you would have the guts to stand against the crowd and do the right thing? Even if people hated you, called you names, and poured drinks on you, you would still be happy because in that moment you would possess a good that is worth immeasurably more than any human honor. But it's really, really hard to go against the crowd, isn't it?

Peter Kreeft once said, "We are conformists. Even non-conformists conform to the fads and fashions of their non-conformity. Rebellious teenagers talk the same, dress the same. They voluntarily don the same uniforms to express their non-conformity. They demand to be honored by their peers above all things." He went on to say, "Honor is prized in every society but the pre-modern version of honor was excellence, being better than anyone else at something. This is still prized but only in the world of entertainment and sports and theaters that we erect to distract ourselves from ourselves."[3]

That brings us to another temptation to happiness found outside of God: fame and glory. Can these things make us happy?

CAN FAME MAKE US HAPPY?

Now you might be wondering, "What's the difference between honor and fame?" You're not alone. In their commentary on Aquinas, Christina Van Dyke and Thomas Williams say that "the most puzzling thing about this article for the contemporary reader is how fame or glory is meant to differ from honor." They point out that Aquinas defines fame or glory as "illustrious" knowledge and corresponding praise, but "we have to first know (or at least think we know) that someone is happy in order to give them glory for it. Like honor, glory is a consequence of happiness, not one of it essential elements."[4]

For our purposes, we can distinguish honor from fame in relation to virtue. Honor is the reward a virtuous person receives, and fame is the reward a "shining" or impressive person receives. There are honorable people who aren't famous (like war veterans) and famous people who aren't honorable (pick

---

[3] Peter Kreeft, *Practical Theology* (San Francisco: Ignatius Press, 2014) electronic edition.

[4] Christina Van Dyke and Thomas Williams, *The Treatise on Happiness,* trans. Thomas Williams (Indianapolis: Hackett Publishing Company, 2016), 230.

any celebrity who is "famous for being famous").

While they differ in important respects, Aquinas' answer will be similar for both: fame can't make us happy because it's an effect of happiness. He writes that "the perfection of human good, which is called happiness, cannot be caused by human knowledge: but rather human knowledge of another's happiness proceeds from, and, in a fashion, is caused by, human happiness itself."[5]

In other words, while God's knowledge causes things to exist, our knowledge is caused by things that exist. And so the idea or the belief that my happiness will be caused by another person's thoughts about me gets things backwards. People can think very highly of me, they can think great things about me, but again, those thoughts still remain in the other person and cannot cause anything in me at all.

I remember when I had one thousand followers on Twitter. I thought, "Dude, that's awesome." And then after a while you look around and say, "Oh man, other people have more followers . . . oh man, I need more followers." Why? Counting followers on Twitter and thinking that's a big deal is sort of like counting Monopoly money and thinking you're rich. I have tens of thousands of followers on Twitter right now, but so what? Other people have millions. Who cares?

Now, there can be an advantage to having followers: if we want to share things, that's great. I think it's good that there are people who are speaking good, truth, and goodness into the world have a large platform. But when we think these things will make us happy—these honors, this recognition, the fact that we might be considered famous by some—Thomas assures

---

[5] *ST* I-II, q. 2, a. 3.

us that we are sorely mistaken.

But if it's true that fame or popularity can't make us happy, then why does it feel good when we know other people like us? Why does Sally Field seem so ecstatic when she accepts her second Academy Award at the 1984 Oscars and exclaims, "I haven't had an orthodox career, and I've wanted more than anything to have your respect. The first time I didn't feel it, but this time I feel it, and I can't deny the fact that you like me, right now, you like me!"

Most people misquote her speech as, "You like me, you really like me," and according to Matthew D. Lieberman in his book *Social: Why Our Brains Are Wired to Connect*, "It isn't just actors who are primarily motivated by being liked; we all are. The misquote is so sticky because it exemplifies a central human need. We all have a need to belong. Signs that others like, admire and love us are central to our well-being."[6]

But it isn't just that admiration we crave. We want people to "really" like us, and not fake it for our benefit. Most of all, we want them to identify something good *in us* that they like. Once again, happiness can't come from outside of us; it has to be found within us. And that leads to the true source of our happiness in our interior lives.

THE INTERIOR LIFE

The interior life is that inner conversation that takes place within yourself when no one is around. It's that inner dialogue that takes place when you lie in bed late at night. This is what

---

[6] Matthew D. Lieberman, *SOCIAL: Why Our Brains Are Wired to Connect* (Oxford: Oxford University Press, 2013), 76.

we mean by the interior life. And of course what that ought to evolve into is not just a conversation with yourself, but a conversation with God. However, when we're distracted from a very young age by electronics and noise and whatever, we can become hindered in this area of our life.

We don't remain inside ourselves because we don't know how to remain inside ourselves, and so we seek to distract ourselves from ourselves because we are not at peace with ourselves. Pascal talks about this in the *Pensées*, and it's one of my favorite quotes from him: "The sole cause of man's unhappiness is that he does not know how to stay quietly in his room. A man wealthy enough for life's needs would never leave home to go to sea or besiege some fortress if he knew how to stay at home and enjoy it."[7]

If you're looking for a test to see how unhappy you are, there you go. Turn the light off, take the ear buds out, and see how long you can sit with yourself. The one thing so many of us find intolerable is just being alone with ourselves. No TV, no computer, no phone. Just our thoughts. Why does that terrify us so much? I think it's because we realize that there's nothing so special about us and that scares us. We're nothing, and so we crave attention or distraction from anyone else to escape the fact. We search social media and the opinions of others: "Do they think highly of me? Do they think I'm someone to be revered? Do they think I'm worth their time? Do they think I'm worth anything at all?"

Now, I promised you in our discussion of pride that I would share with you the Litany of Humility. Some of you know what it is and you pray it; others of you don't. And for those

---

[7]   Pascal, *Pensées*, §37.

of you who don't, boy am I pumped to share it with you. If you don't think that you're one of these people that we've been talking about who wants the praise and recognition of others, that's either because you're a saint or maybe a little deluded. Either way, this prayer will bring those illusions to the surface. Here it is:

O Jesus! meek and humble of heart, **Hear me.**
From the desire of being esteemed,
Deliver me, Jesus.

From the desire of being loved . . .
From the desire of being extolled . . .
From the desire of being honored . . .
From the desire of being praised . . .
From the desire of being preferred to others . . .
From the desire of being consulted . . .
From the desire of being approved . . .
From the fear of being humiliated . . .
From the fear of being despised . . . .
From the fear of suffering rebukes . . .
From the fear of being calumniated . . .
From the fear of being forgotten . . .
From the fear of being ridiculed . . .
From the fear of being wronged . . .
From the fear of being suspected . . .

That others may be loved more than I,
Jesus, grant me the grace to desire it.

That others may be esteemed more than I . . .
That, in the opinion of the world, others may

increase and I may decrease . . .
That others may be chosen and I set aside . . .
That others may be praised and I unnoticed . . .
That others may be preferred to me in everything . . .
That others may become holier than I, provided that
I may become as holy as I should . . .

If you pray this every day, and you mean what you say, that's going to bless you and it's going to bless me a great deal too. And now that we know what won't make us happy, it's time to turn to the treasures God gave us that lead to happiness in this life and prepare us for perfect happiness in the next life.

SECTION 3

WHAT *WILL* MAKE US HAPPY

7.

PRUDENT "MORAL MUSCLES"

HAVE YOU EVER TRIED TO EXERCISE with a friend or play a game like basketball and realize you're totally out of shape or you just "don't have it anymore?" It's kind of weird, if you think about it.

Let's say you used to be great at basketball. You know how to sink those three-pointers but you've been busy with the new job and your kids have started school, and so you haven't picked up the ball in years. Then, your irritatingly chipper childless buddy comes back from the gym and wants to shoot hoops with you and, even though you sink a few, your friend just destroys you. Why?

You know in your head how to line up the shot and sink the basket, but when you haven't done it in a while, there's a disconnect between getting your body to execute what your mind and will want to do. Your "muscle memory" deteriorates and you lose the reflexive response you once had in these situations. The same thing happens to us in our moral lives when we fail to practice virtue.

MORAL MUSCLE MEMORY

We end up getting into the same fights with our spouse and kids (or even total strangers) or falling into the same past sins because, even though we make a firm resolution to "sin no more," we haven't developed the "moral muscle memory" that reflexively pushes us to do good when we're tempted to do evil. And because we end up acting against reason and choosing evil when we should choose good, we lose out on the happiness God wants for us.

That's why Aquinas says that whatever happiness we can find in this life must ultimately come from developing virtue, which he defines as follows: "Virtue is a good quality of the mind, by which we live righteously, of which no one can make bad use, which God works in us, without us."[1]

Aquinas notes that while we can think badly of the virtues (like that they're stupid and unnecessary), we can't act badly with them. If we truly practice the virtues, then we can't do evil because they are ordered through reason towards the good. He also notes that a subset of these virtues that we will discuss in the next chapter, called the infused virtues, come directly from God through our free cooperation. But for right now I want to focus on the acquired virtues, which anyone can attain through exercising the moral sense that God gave us (though it often requires God's grace, regardless). The *Catechism* gives a good definition of virtue that also applies to this set of them:

> A virtue is an habitual and firm disposition to do the good. It allows the person not only to perform good acts, but to give the best of himself. The virtuous per-

---

[1] *ST* I-II, q. 55, a. 4.

son tends toward the good with all his sensory and spiritual powers; he pursues the good and chooses it in concrete actions. (1803)

Aquinas lists a lot of virtues but four of them are the "hinge" upon which all the other virtues rest. These are the cardinal virtues (*cardo* is Latin for "hinge") of prudence, justice, temperance, and courage, which refer to finding the good, giving that which is good to others, aiming our passions towards the good, and removing fear that keeps us from choosing the good.

PRUDENCE

Have you ever known someone who *seems* to be really holy but they end up annoying you because they are so out of touch with the world? These people always remember to say their daily Rosary or go to Mass, but then they say uncomfortable things to people or just can't seem to relate to them.

What these people have in common is that they lack the virtue of prudence, or the ability to use reason in order to achieve the good. Aquinas says that "prudence is wisdom about human affairs: but not wisdom absolutely, because it is not about the absolutely highest cause, for it is about human good, and this is not the best thing of all."[2]

If theology and philosophy are "book smarts," or knowledge about the most important things we should care about (like God), then prudence involves "street smarts," or how to navigate the world in order to achieve various goods. You shouldn't confuse prudence with the craftiness of a con artist, who knows how to manipulate people into giving him what he wants. As

---

[2] *ST* II-II, q. 47, a. 2.

Stephen Pope explains, that's not the kind of "street smarts" Aquinas is talking about:

> Prudence is not defined as simply finding the best means to any end whatsoever, as the false prudence of the "good crook" or the "worldly wise." As a moral virtue, it takes its bearings from the good. It reflects not only on the end of this or that act (as, for example, how to treat justly a needy but dishonest employee) but also about how all of one's acts considered as a whole fit into the end of human life.[3]

So we might say Danny Ocean in the heist film *Oceans 11* is a "good thief" in the sense that he is crafty and good at beating casino security. But this is far different from Dismas, the "good thief" on the cross who asked Jesus to remember him when he enters his kingdom (Luke 23:42). Aristotle says, "It is impossible for a man to be prudent unless he be good"[4] because prudence is about finding the right way to achieve *the* good, not just what someone thinks is good (like walking away with 150 million dollars of casino money that isn't yours).

Prudence makes us happy because it helps us avoid hazards and bad situations that take away our happiness. It also provides us the smoothest path to the things that make us happy. But how do we grow in prudence? We can do that by remembering that prudence rests on a three-step path of counsel, judgment, and command.

When I chose to leave Catholic Answers in order to focus

---

[3] Stephen J. Pope, "Overview of the Ethics of Thomas Aquinas," in *The Ethics of Aquinas,* ed. Stephen J. Pope (Washington, DC: Georgetown University Press, 2002), 40.

[4] *ST* II-II, q. 47, a. 13.

on my anti-pornography work, I knew it might either be my biggest relief or my biggest regret. So before I stood up at my desk and said, "I'm outta here, suckers!" I first sought counsel. Through counsel we gather facts and use them to guide us to the correct conclusion, or a sound *judgment*.

What were the realistic things I stood to gain in choosing to depart from Catholic Answers? What could I realistically expect to lose? What were the costs involved in the decision? Could my family and I *pay* those costs (financial, emotional, spiritual)? Sometimes we can use our own reasoning to seek this counsel on our own, but it usually helps to seek the counsel of others as well. That's why Scripture says, "Without counsel plans go wrong, but with many advisers they succeed" (Prov 15:22).

Finally, once we have our judgment, we must *command* the will to follow through. (What, you've never chickened out even when you had the best choice right in front of you?)

When we practice these steps, we develop the other perfections that rely on prudence, like memory (remembering what works and what doesn't), docility (being open to the advice of others), shrewdness (being able to intuitively sense how things ought to go), foresight (predicting how actions will play out), circumspection (the ability to take all circumstances into account), and caution (the ability to know when delay is preferable to action, even in good circumstances).

Ultimately, prudence isn't something that can be learned quickly in academic study like a new language or code. It's something that we develop at a deeper level through our own experiences. So when you colossally fail at something, remember that this is God's way of helping you grow in prudence by showing you the consequence of being imprudent.

That's why almost every culture on earth has revered elders as being sources of wisdom—they've been around long enough to learn from their own mistakes and usually want to keep us from doing the same. That's why the Bible tells us, "Wisdom is with the aged, and understanding in length of days. With God are wisdom and might; he has counsel and understanding" (Job 12:12–13).

But there are some simple things we can do to grow in prudence, and it's important to make the effort. The *Catechism* calls prudence the *"auriga virtutum"* ("the charioteer of the virtues"), because prudence

> guides the other virtues by setting rule and measure. It is prudence that immediately guides the judgment of conscience. The prudent man determines and directs his conduct in accordance with this judgment. With the help of this virtue we apply moral principles to particular cases without error and overcome doubts about the good to achieve and the evil to avoid. (1806)

GROWING IN PRUDENCE

One way to grow in prudence is to recognize where we tend to act imprudently. Aquinas says there are three common culprits behind these kinds of behaviors: impulse, passion, and stubbornness.[5]

---

[5] Edward P. Sri, "The Art of Living: The First Step of Prudence," *Lay Witness* (May/June 2009). Available online at https://www.catholic-ducation.org/en/culture/catholic-contributions/the-art-of-living-the-first-step-of-prudence.html.

Impulse causes us to "leap before we look"; we have a surge of energy and think, "that's a great idea!" But we don't take time to use our God-given intellect and do something nonhuman animals cannot do: map out the consequences of our actions. I understand the temptation to be impulsive, especially on social media. You feel like if you have a great thought, you have to be the first one to get it out there into the world so you can receive praise from other people. Or you're at a party and the best joke or juiciest story about someone else pops into your little brain and you have to share it so, once again, you get that sweet, sweet hit of praise from others.

Notice a pattern here?

In order to grow in prudence (as well as happiness), practice each day saying something like, "I'm going to think this over." Now this can lead to the extreme of overanalyzing a situation and never acting at all, which is also imprudent, but I think a lot of us make ourselves miserable more by what we do than by what we fail to do. In those cases, we should just take a moment and practice in short bits a delayed response.

Want to post something on the Internet? Wait an hour and see if it's still a good idea. Do you really want to buy that expensive treat in the store? Wait until tomorrow and see if you still want it. The more we do this, the more we see that life isn't a race to be happy RIGHT NOW. It's a journey towards happiness that relies not on getting there quickly but on getting there carefully. You're not sprinting to the end of the 100-yard dash; this is a hike up what can be a beautiful yet treacherous mountain.

So take the time to plan your route and enjoy the scenery!

Now, the second cause of imprudent behavior is passion, or

getting swept away in our emotions. In the *Summa* Thomas makes a distinction between being responsible for passions we directly cause and those which spring up within us apart from our control. He writes that

> because a passion is sometimes so strong as to take away the use of reason altogether, as in the case of those who are mad through love or anger; and then if such a passion were voluntary from the beginning, the act is reckoned a sin, because it is voluntary in its cause, as we have stated with regard to drunkenness [or drinking with the intent of becoming drunk]. If, however, the cause be not voluntary but natural, for instance, if anyone through sickness or some such cause fall into such a passion as deprives him of the use of reason, his act is rendered wholly involuntary, and he is entirely excused from sin.[6]

In some cases, we might have a passion that comes from a physical or mental illness that keeps us from being rational, and in those cases we should seek competent psychiatric care. In other cases, we might be so overcome by grief or anger that we do something sinful, but our responsibility for sin is diminished. This is also why the law makes a distinction between killing in the heat of the moment (manslaughter) and killing that is premeditated (murder).

Now, that does *not* mean we aren't responsible for sins just because we had a surge of emotion before they happened. We aren't animals; we can control our passions, it just takes practice and prudence. So, for example, if there is a situation where you know beforehand that you're likely to "blow a fuse" or

---

[6] *ST* I-II, q. 77, a. 7.

do something sinful, prudently exercise foresight and remove those temptations.

Take extra snacks so hunger doesn't tempt you be a glutton or a wrathful tyrant. When you feel like exploding in anger or engaging in a private sin like masturbation, remove yourself from the situation so you don't have to use your willpower on simply "not sinning." Instead, work on using your willpower for something positive, like developing an alternative to the imprudent behavior. For example, instead of working to avoid wrath, work to calmly yet assertively discipline your children.

And most importantly, when (not if) you fail, use it as an opportunity to plan out how things will be different next time. This brings us to the third cause of imprudent behavior: stubbornness. Aquinas gives a good breakdown of four common reasons people fall into stubbornness and end up making imprudent decisions:

> First, as regards the intellect, and thus we have "obstinacy," by which a man is too much attached to his own opinion, being unwilling to believe one that is better. Secondly, as regards the will, and then we have "discord," whereby a man is unwilling to give up his own will, and agree with others. Thirdly, as regards "speech," and then we have "contention," whereby a man quarrels noisily with another. Fourthly as regards deeds, and this is "disobedience," whereby a man refuses to carry out the command of his superiors.[7]

All the reasons for stubbornness have roughly the same cause: we love something of ours more than what other people

---

[7] *ST* II-II, q. 132, a. 5.

(including God) would like to give us. We think our beliefs, decisions, and actions are always better than others, and if we maintain that attitude, we are on the express train to pride town. The best advice I have for the stubborn person is to appeal to their nobility: you are too smart to be stubborn!

I once read a book on marriage that said when wives correct their husbands, they shouldn't try to make them feel small. Instead, they should say things like, "Stop being such a big brute!" The idea here is that we should see that living a virtuous life isn't just something we do because we have to; it's something we should do because we want to be happy and we want to stop buying the fake means to happiness the world and our sinful nature keep trying to sell us.

8.

TEMPERATE, JUST COURAGE

WHEN MY WIFE, CAMERON, was a teenager, she attended a party where the parents weren't home. She, along with almost everyone else, was either drunk or close to it.

There was one young man named Charlie, however, who was a Christian and so, being underage, had chosen not to drink. At one point during the party, Charlie saw a young man approach Cameron. He saw the man support Cameron with his arms and begin to lead her upstairs. It was at this point Charlie had a decision to make.

Would he wimp out and say something pathetic like "live and let live"? Or would he man up and protect his friend? Thankfully he chose the latter.

Charlie intercepted them at the staircase and asked the guy, "What are you doing?"

The man responded, "We're going up to the bedroom, what do you think we're doing? Get out of the way."

At this point, Charlie pushed his finger into the man's chest and said, "Yeah, not gonna happen." The young man dropped Cameron's arm and backed away. Charlie then walked Cameron up the stairs and laid her down on a bed. He took a pillow for himself, exited the room, closed the door, and slept across the doorway.

Why? If that young man wanted to come back for Cameron, he'd have to get through Charlie first. Can you imagine the amount of respect I have for that guy? Virtues like temperance, courage, and a proper sense of justice are admirable and praiseworthy and it's to those virtues we turn now.

TEMPERANCE

Throughout his writings on the virtues, Aristotle often uses the phrase, "in the middle between" to denote a well-known Greek concept that would later be called "the golden mean" and summarized in the saying, "nothing to excess." In other words, you should try to stay on the middle ground and not take things to extremes. The earliest articulation of this theme can be found in the story of Icarus, whose father, Daedalus, made him wings to help him escape the rule of the Cretan King Minos. His father told him to "fly the middle course" between the spray of the ocean and the heat of the sun that would melt his wings. Icarus failed to heed the warning, and that led to him crashing into the ocean and drowning.

One of the objections Aquinas deals with when it comes to the idea of temperance being a virtue is that virtues are supposed to correspond to nature, but it seems like temperance always tells us that certain natural things, like food, drink, and sex, are unnatural and should be avoided. Aquinas responds by pointing out that "temperance is not contrary to the inclination of human nature, but is in accord with it. It is, however, contrary to the inclination of the animal nature that is not subject to reason."[1]

This reminds me of when people say things like, "Homosexuality is perfectly natural. There are dozens of animal species that practice it!" Well, sure, but animals also forcibly copulate with each other (rape for humans) and kill each other for food and shelter (murder for humans). We are animals, and so we have the same natural desires for food and intercourse as other animals, but because we have immortal souls, we also have distinctly human desires to live in accordance with reason. That means we still seek out these basic needs, but we seek them as a means to achieve higher ends as rational creatures, and not as ends in and of themselves.

The cardinal virtues can be described as finding the "middle path" between extremes, but Aquinas sees temperance as a special case of this middle path rooted in the restraining of our bodily passions. He says temperance is one of the most important virtues because "these [bodily] pleasures are most natural to us, so that it is more difficult to abstain from them, and to control the desire for them, and because their objects are more necessary to the present life."[2]

Unfortunately, some of us do act like animals and seek these things as our highest end or goal in life. St. Paul said of people in this sad condition, "many, of whom I have often told you and now tell you even with tears, walk as enemies of the cross of Christ. Their end is destruction, their god is the belly, and they glory in their shame, with minds set on earthly things" (Phil 3:18–19).

---

[1]   *ST* II-II, q. 141, a. 1.
[2]   *ST* II-II, q. 141, a. 7.

However, remember the middle path! We shouldn't act like gluttonous, lustful beasts, but we also shouldn't reject all bodily pleasures as being sinful. Even ascetics, or those who withdraw from the pleasures of the world so they can be closer to God, don't consider bodily pleasures to be evil. Those pleasures are simply less good than the pleasures that come from contemplating God.

Now, while temperance is a great virtue, it's not the greatest of the virtues. St. Gregory of Nyssa says, "The goal of a virtuous life is to become like God." Temperance grants us perfection in relation to *things*, but the other virtues grant us perfection in relation to *persons*. And this makes us more like God, who makes us perfect as he is perfect (Matt 5:48). That's why Aquinas quotes Aristotle, who says that the "greatest virtues are those which are most profitable to others, for which reason we give the greatest honor to the brave and the just."[3]

JUSTICE

When you think of the virtues, you might not think of justice as one of them. I mean, isn't justice something that falls under the duties of policemen, judges, and Batman? Why should you and I care about justice, and how does this virtue make us happier people?

Aquinas says that justice "directs man in his relations with other men," and he distinguishes between the concepts of legal justice and virtuous justice. Unlike the other virtues, which aim to make us good people, legal justice makes us good citizens and protects the common good of society. But there is a

---

[3] *ST* II-II, q. 141, a. 8.

sense in which justice makes us good people because it helps us give our neighbor what "he is due."

In one passage Aquinas answers the following objection: As long as I follow the law and practice legal justice, why do I need to go the extra mile and practice justice beyond what the law requires? For example, as long as I pay social security taxes and don't steal money from my parents, aren't I giving them "what they are due" and satisfying the virtue of justice without additional acts of charity towards them?

Clearly, following the law is a minimum standard for morality, not the fulfillment of it. In another passage Aquinas says that the state cannot and should not pass a law to mandate every single moral obligation because that would create greater evils than those the law is trying to abolish. Can you imagine if there was a department of promise keeping? So the law provides a minimum standard of morality and helps us promote society as a whole, but this general kind of justice only aids individuals *indirectly*.

We are also called to prudently determine what we owe to other people in virtue of their being human beings in relation to us. Of course this differs among human beings because we are not called to treat all of our relationships as being equal to one another. My duty to my children outranks my duty towards strangers, but if I can feed a poor stranger without depriving my children of food, then I am obliged to do that when it is reasonable for me to do so. It also helps me know when to say "no" to people because in saying yes I might be neglecting my primary responsibilities (such as volunteering on a long-term project for a friend when this would cause me to be away from family too much). Jean Porter offers a nice summary in her book on Aquinas and the virtue of justice:

General and particular justice work together in such a way as to direct the agent rightly toward the human good—nothing more, since any higher good would be the province of charity, but also nothing less, and nothing else. Justice perfects men and women by humanizing them, in the fullest sense, orienting them rightly toward one another and the human world they share.[4]

COURAGE

A few years ago I agreed to debate a pornographic film producer and actress (or, to put it bluntly, a pornographer and a porn star) on the subject, "Is pornography harmful?" As I prepared for the debate and told others about it, some people told me, "Wow, it's really brave of you to publicly challenge people like that." But I was super nervous and thinking, "Yep, I probably got way in over my head but here goes nothing!"

I was not the "calm, cool, collected" person you might think can engage in a high-stress situation like that. But guess what? Nobody who is courageous has a complete absence of fear. In fact, the golden mean helps us distinguish the true virtue of courage from its common imposter, foolhardiness.

The courageous person and the foolhardy person might both charge headfirst into a dangerous situation in order to do good (like rescue people trapped in a burning building), but unlike the truly courageous person, the foolhardy person doesn't know how dangerous the situation really is. Aquinas says this false kind of courage manifests itself when a person

---

[4] Jean Porter, *Justice as a Virtue: A Thomistic Perspective* (Grand Rapids, MI: Wm. B. Eerdmans, 2016), 116.

is "not perceiving the greatness of the danger" that lies ahead of them.[5] This can happen because of ignorance or because they are blinded by their passions (like when an angry soldier charges enemy lines to avenge his fallen comrades).

The point is that courage (or what is traditionally called fortitude) is not about being fearless. Aquinas says courage is the virtue that "remove[s] any obstacle that withdraws the will from following the reason . . . fortitude is about fear and daring, as curbing fear and moderating daring."[6]

I love that—fear and daring. It takes guts to be a good person in an evil world. We can read all the philosophical treatises in the world that tell us how to live a good life, but at the end of the day we can always hit the "moral snooze button" on our conscience when it tries to get us to do the right thing.

One definition of fear I like is this: the feeling a creature feels when it thinks its needs won't be met. I get annoyed when I have to wait a while at a traffic light but I don't *need* to be going anywhere at that moment. Yet when I see a car barreling towards me as it runs a red light, I feel that twinge of fear and my *need* to not be cocooned in a twisted pile of metal that could catch on fire becomes fully present to me.

So ask yourself, "What do we think we *need* that makes us afraid to practice these basic virtues?" Do I *need* that bodily pleasure from food or drink? Am I really going to die if I don't have that dessert or alcohol that I think will bring me true contentment? Do I *need* that extra bit of cash that I'm thinking about not giving to the poor or will my life be basically the same without? Finally, do I *need* people's approval so much

---

[5]   *ST* II-II, q. 123, a. 1.
[6]   *ST* II-II, q. 123, a. 3.

that I'm afraid to share my love of Jesus with them?

When we trust that God has won the ultimate victory over death, we no longer have any reason to be afraid of what happens to us in this life. I love when St. John tells us, "There is no fear in love, but perfect love casts out fear. For fear has to do with punishment, and he who fears is not perfected in love" (1 John 4:18).

The virtues are God's way of perfecting us in love and it is through the life of virtue that we see that the pleasures of this world can't bring us perpetual peace: only God can do that. As St. Paul said, "I have learned, in whatever state I am, to be content. I know how to be abased, and I know how to abound; in any and all circumstances I have learned the secret of facing plenty and hunger, abundance and want. I can do all things in him who strengthens me" (Phil 4:11–13).

9.

FAITH, HOPE, AND LOVE

WE'VE SEEN HOW THE CARDINAL VIRTUES help us to live
in accordance with our nature (how God made us), and so
they produce happiness at least in this life. But ultimately we
weren't made for this life alone. We don't have a purely natural
end. Our hearts long for an endless happiness that does not
exist in this life except in shadows or "foretastes" of what is
to come. The only way we can attain eternal life with God is
through the grace he gives us, which is why faith, hope, and
love are called theological virtues.

We can't merit these virtues on our own; we can only accept
God's gift of them to us. We can definitely ask God for them,
and predispose ourselves to receive them by practicing the cardinal virtues, but when we do receive that gift, it is because God
has been gracious to us, not because we worked really hard for
them. Anyone can have these virtues in a common, "earthly"
way, but it is only through God that we can exercise these virtues in a way that draws us closer to him and the supreme happiness he wants for us. Bonnie Kent puts it this way:

> While naturally acquired moral virtues make people
> well suited to the human affairs and earthly happi-

ness that concern all—because we are all human—infused moral virtues make people well suited to the life Christians must live because they are Christians: persons belonging to the household of God, with love of God as the highest good, faith in God's word, and hope for the happiness of the afterlife.[1]

KEEP THE FAITH

When I share content about God or Aquinas on the Internet, some atheists give me a snarky reply about the uselessness of faith. They say religion isn't built on reason but on "faith," and that if we actually had evidence for what we believed, then we wouldn't need faith. When I ask them to define what they mean by the word "faith," I often get answers like "believing without evidence" or even "believing in spite of what the evidence says."

For these people, faith is just wishful thinking at best or a dangerous delusion at worst. But everybody has faith in the common sense of that word. The *Cambridge English Dictionary* defines faith as "a high degree of trust or confidence in something or someone."

We all have faith in the people who build our bridges, make our food, and prescribe our medicine. Sometimes that faith is misplaced and those people fail us, but that doesn't mean faith itself is irrational. It just means we should carefully discern the objects of our faith, and there can be no more trustworthy an object for our faith than God, who is truth itself. In fact, Aquinas would say it's irrational to *not* have faith in God, because

---

[1] Bonnie Kent, "Habits and Virtues," in *The Ethics of Aquinas,* 122.

that is the means by which we can have true happiness in this life. He writes that

> faith is said to be the "substance of things to be hoped for," for the reason that in us the first beginning of things to be hoped for is brought about by the assent of faith, which contains virtually all things to be hoped for. Because we hope to be made happy through seeing the unveiled truth to which our faith cleaves, as was made evident when we were speaking of happiness.[2]

Think of faith as having that "light bulb moment" where we understand that God is real and wants us to have eternal life with him. Jesus said that we don't need very much faith to have this kind of moment; an amount as small as a mustard seed would suffice (Matt 17:20). And this seed of faith contains virtually all the happiness waiting for us when we encounter God face-to-face in the next life. It is like how a tiny embryo contains a child's physical characteristics within its DNA and through time these characteristics will become more and more manifest.

Faith isn't just about having the right beliefs about God or having the right "answers." It's about being united to God by understanding the truth of who he is. That's why Aquinas says, "Faith has the character of a virtue, not because of the things it believes, for faith is of things that appear not, but because it adheres to the testimony of one in whom truth is infallibly found."[3]

---

[2] *ST* II-II, q. 4, a. 1.

[3] Aquinas, *De veritate*, q. 14, a. 8.

Faith is the key that puts every other truth into its proper place. Triumphs become opportunities for gratitude instead of pride. Tragedies become opportunities for growth instead of despair. Life just makes more sense and our faith in God gives us joy even when we face what can feel like insurmountable trials. Thomas Schmidt provides a powerful example of this in his book, *A Scandalous Beauty*. He describes how he once went to a nursing home to bring flowers to the patients there and he came across an eighty-nine-year-old woman named Mabel. Here's how he tells it:

> As I neared the end of the hallway, I saw an old woman strapped up in a wheelchair. Her face was a horror. The empty stare and white pupils of her eyes told me that she was blind. The large hearing aid over one ear told me that she was almost deaf. One side of her face was being eaten by cancer. There was a discolored and running sore covering part of one cheek, and it had pushed her nose to one side, dropped one eye, and distorted her jaw so that what should have been the corner of her mouth was the bottom of her mouth. As a consequence, she drooled constantly. I was told later that when new aides arrived, the supervisors would send them to feed this woman, thinking that if they could stand this sight they could stand anything in the building. I also learned later that this woman was eighty-nine years old and that she had been here, bed-ridden, blind, nearly deaf, and alone, for twenty-five years. This was Mabel.

How would you feel if you were Mabel? I know I couldn't even fathom the kind of person I'd become if I had to endure this much suffering; I wouldn't be surprised if I crumbled and became a depressed or angry person. But that wasn't the case for Mabel. When Schmidt asked her what she thought about during all those years she spent in darkness and pain, she simply said, "I think about my Jesus." And then she sang a hymn:

> Jesus is all the world to me
> My life, my joy, my all.
> He is my strength from day to day
> Without him I would fall
> When I am sad, to him I go, No other one can cheer me so.
> When I am sad, he makes me glad.
> He's my friend.

Schmidt then emphatically tells his readers:

> *This is not fiction.* Incredible as it may seem, a human being really lived like this. I know. I knew her. I watched her for three years. How could she do it? Seconds ticked and minutes crawled, and so did days and weeks and months and years of pain without human company and without an explanation of why it was all happening—and she lay there and sang hymns. How could she do it? The answer, I think, is that Mabel had something that you and I don't have much of. She had power. Lying there in that bed, unable to move, unable to see, unable to hear, unable to talk to anyone, she had incredible power.[4]

That, my friends, is the power of faith. However, faith can only become this mature and this powerful when it is joined to

---

[4] Thomas Schmidt, *A Scandalous Beauty: The Artistry of God and the Way of the Cross* (Ada, MI: Brazos Press, 2002), 86–88.

another virtue that sustains it: the virtue of hope.

HERE'S HOPING

A lot of people think faith and hope are basically the same thing but there's a crucial difference between the two. Let me borrow an example from the Christian apologist Timothy McGrew. Suppose you go skydiving and you have good evidence that your parachute has been packed properly and that you have everything you need to make it safely to the ground. But even with all this evidence you still have to make the decision to trust that evidence and jump out of the plane.

You have to take that "leap of faith."

McGrew says that if all he had was the "hope" that he would make it safely to the ground, then he would keep his behind firmly planted in his seat and not jump. That's because in this case hope is an expression of what he supremely desires (which is to not free-fall all the way to the ground). But without any reason to think that what is hoped for will come to pass, then hope is not very hopeful. Instead, hope has to be conjoined with faith in order to provide someone with the perseverance to wait for what they desire even if the path to that ultimate end is difficult.

So, for our skydiving example, you have faith you will safely make it to the ground and this reinforces your hope that you will make it there. This corresponds to how the author of the Letter to the Hebrews understands the relationship between faith and hope. He writes, "Now faith is the assurance of things hoped for, the conviction of things not seen" (Heb 11:1). Aquinas says of hope, "the object of hope is a future good, difficult but possible to obtain . . . in so far as we hope for anything as being possible to us by means of the Divine assistance, our hope attains God Himself, on Whose help it leans."[5]

We don't hope for things that we know will happen or for things that are bad for us. For example, I don't hope I will die, but rather I hope I will *not* die. Or at least when I do die, I hope it will be a "good death," where I am prepared to enter into eternity with God and leave this life in the presence of my loved ones. Conversely, when we die and enter into God's embrace in heaven, we will no longer possess the virtues of either faith or hope because what we believed and hoped for will be immediately present to us. As St. Paul said, "For now we see in a mirror dimly, but then face to face. Now I know in part; then I shall understand fully, even as I have been fully understood" (1 Cor 13:12).

While faith unites us to God as the ultimate truth we should believe, hope unites us to God as the ultimate good to which we should order our lives. So while we do hope for things in this life, like getting an A on a school assignment, hope in the proper sense as a virtue relates to our striving towards God himself. Aquinas says that "we should hope from Him for nothing less than Himself, since His goodness, whereby He imparts good things to His creature, is no less than His Essence. Therefore the proper and principal object of hope is eternal happiness."[6]

To make another analogy, if our souls are like a candle that enables us to shine a light into the world (see Matt 5:14), then faith is the match that lights the candle and hope is the wax that sustains it and allows our light to grow brighter over

---

[5] *ST* II-II, q. 17, a. 1.
[6] *ST* II-II, q. 17, a. 2.

time. Aquinas says that while the worst sins, strictly speaking, are those against justice, the most dangerous sins are those against hope. That's because "hope withdraws us from evils and induces us to seek for good things, so that when hope is given up, men rush headlong into sin, and are drawn away from good works."[7]

Hope is especially important when we reach the limit of the natural happiness that flows from the cardinal virtues we discussed earlier. Even when we practice temperance, prudence, courage, and justice, life can just really, *suck* (I believe "suck" is a fine word to use in a philosophical discourse). In those cases, hope is what keeps our eyes affixed to the true happiness that surpasses everything we endure in this life. St. Paul put it well:

> [W]e do not lose heart. Though our outer man is wasting away, our inner man is being renewed every day. For this slight momentary affliction is preparing for us an eternal weight of glory beyond all comparison, because we look not to the things that are seen but to the things that are unseen; for the things that are seen are transient, but the things that are unseen are eternal. (2 Cor 4:16–18)

Fr. Philip Bochanski, who has written a wonderful book on the virtue of hope, says that while the cardinal virtues are primarily about the relationships we have with other people, the theological virtues reflect our relationship with God. He says:

> Hope is premised on the notion that I am not self-sufficient, that there are things that I cannot ever do completely on my own, and that I ought to look

---

[7] *ST* II-II, q. 20, a. 3.

trustingly to God for help. So, humility is absolutely essential—prideful people who are the center of their own universe delude themselves that they have no need to look anywhere else for guidance or assistance, and thus no reason to hope. Hope is the way to true humility, as we learn to trust ourselves less precisely because we are learning to trust God more, and learning that we can trust God infinitely.[8]

THE GREATEST OF THESE IS LOVE

When people hear about the theological virtues, they can understand how something like faith, or even hope, can only come from God. But some people may take offense at the idea that love (what is traditionally called charity) is a theological virtue. Why isn't it a cardinal virtue? Is Aquinas saying that only Christians can truly love other people or practice charity?

Just as anyone can exercise the common notions of faith and hope, anyone can practice love in the general sense of willing the good for another person. Jesus pointed out that even evil people are good at loving people who care about them (Matt 5:46). Instead, Aquinas tells us that the theological virtue of love involves not just willing the good for others but willing *the good itself*—in other words, God. He writes:

> Augustine says: "Charity is a virtue which, when our affections are perfectly ordered, unites us to God, for by it we love Him." . . . [J]ust as moral virtue is

---

[8] Kathryn Jean Lopez, "Could You Use Some Hope?" *National Review,* August 10, 2019. Available online at https://www.nationalreview.com/2019/08/father-philip-bochanski-the-virtue-of-hope/.

defined as being "in accord with right reason," so too, the nature of virtue consists in attaining God, as also stated above with regard to faith, and hope. Wherefore, it follows that charity is a virtue, for, since charity attains God, it unites us to God.[9]

Aquinas also says that faith and hope precede charity in the sense of generation because "it is by faith that the intellect apprehends the object of hope," and "for the very reason that a man hopes in someone, he proceeds to love him." And so faith and hope lead us to have charity, or genuine love for God. But charity precedes faith and hope in the order of perfection because "both faith and hope are quickened [supported] by charity, and receive from charity their full complement as virtues. For thus charity is the mother and the root of all the virtues."[10]

---

[9] *ST* II-II, q. 23, a. 3.

[10] *ST* I-II, q. 62, a. 4.

SECTION 4

GROUNDING
OUR HAPPINESS

10.

CONTROLLING
OUR PASSIONS

SO FAR WE'VE SEEN that our happiness primarily derives from living a life of virtue in accordance with God's design for us. But there is an element of happiness in life that doesn't come from our habitual dispositions but from our reflexive response to whatever life throws at us. It's the feeling we get when our children run into our arms, when we look at a picture of a deceased loved one, or when we see police lights in our rear-view mirror signaling us to pull over. They are our emotions (or what are also called "passions"), and Aquinas says there are four principle ones that we encounter in our lives: joy, sorrow, hope, fear.

But emotions are wily things, so that's why I wanted to share with you an interview I did with Fr. Gregory Pine that will really help us understand our emotions and how they contribute to our happiness in this life:

Matt: When we think of the emotions, I can see two extremes. On one end, you have Stoicism, which looks at emotions as being bad things to always avoid or repress. On the other end of the spectrum you have people who just say, "Go with your emotions. Shun pain. Pursue pleasure." Then you've got Aquinas somewhere in the middle, right?

Fr. Pine: St. Thomas doesn't have a theory of emotion that entails repression or suppression. It's not about only appealing to the will and white-knuckling your way through life, like "Well, you really want food? You need to batten down the hatches and just fast until such time as you're holier."

St. Thomas recognizes that the passions are just movements of our sense appetite. There are things out there in the world that we recognize as fitting for us, whether it be food or drink, which build up our individual life, or sexual intercourse, which builds up the life of the species and hands on our existence, or whatever other things that we find pleasant, be they music or play or liturgy. These things appeal to us in a sensory way, and they beget in us an inclination or an appetite.

We're not only made for reproduction, growth, and nutrition, so we aren't animals who only have sense, cognition, appetite, and movement. We're also blessed with an intellect and a will, which are most constitutive of what it means to be a human. For St. Thomas, it's essential that the passions be incorporated into a truly human life, which entails the judgment and the dictates of reason and the ordering of will, and ultimately that our minds and hearts are illumined by the law of God.

When they're put in their proper place, our passions allow us to enjoy the objects of those desires more than previously because we want what is good, and we want it in the right way, and we want it according to the right measure. We're no longer threatened by the vehemence of our passions, but rather they've come to be trained, ordered, healed, purified, actually empowered and emboldened, in a truly virtuous life.

Matt: I just got the thought of a fire. A fire is good when it is in its place, namely, the fireplace. It is not good when it's on the carpet and burning down the living room.

Fr. Pine: Yes, I agree wholeheartedly. There was once a time, it was in our third house, when we lit a fire. This might be slightly traumatic, but here goes. We lit a fire in the fireplace, and then we heard these terrible scratching sounds. Then we saw the little hand and foot prints of a squirrel in the smoked glass in the front of the fireplace. We just swung the door open, and that guy just ran around our house for a little bit. There was a distinct possibility of him having a burning bushy tail, and then we would have burning valances, but at that point he was just sooty, so it all worked out. Yeah, a burning carpet is a distinct possibility, and we don't want that.

Matt: So the passions are good when they are in accord with reason, and not good when they're not.

Fr. Pine: Yes, the passions are good when they are not squirrels with burning tails.

Matt: And there are four principle emotions: joy, sorrow, hope, fear. Let's break those down.

Fr. Pine: St. Thomas will talk about how we can only ever choose what is apprehended as good, because that's the only thing that motivates us. For instance, when St. Thomas describes the good, he says, "We call those things good which men desire." Basically, what is it to be good? It's to be something that is desirable.

There are two basic responses to that which is good. There's love, which is the recognition of something seen as fitting or that begets in me a kind of complacency. It's a spontaneous recognition of what is out there as somehow for me. Then on the flip side, there is hatred, which is the inverse, the spontaneous recognition of something out there as against me or something unfitting for me or that would otherwise threaten me.

Then from these two basic responses there flow further responses. In the case of love, once you have made the recognition of this thing out there as fitting, if it's not present to you, it begets in you a movement towards the thing itself, and this we call desire. But if it is present to you, or once it becomes present to you, then it begets in you the kind of experience of rest in the thing loved, and this St. Thomas will call *delectatio*, like "delectation," or pleasure, or in the more spiritual sense, joy, *gaudium*.

Matt: So joy is what we feel when we possess the good, but what about when the good is far off?

Fr. Pine: If we recognize something as good and difficult, but worthy of pursuit, Aquinas says that begets in us hope. Here we're not thinking of hope in the sense of the theological virtue, though there is a deep connection between the passion of hope and the virtue of hope. Basically, all hope says is that there is something out there that I have not yet obtained or I have not yet achieved that is good for me. To achieve it will be arduous, but I am also willing to supply the moral energy that it entails to attain that thing. It's a movement towards a good thing, with the recognition that I will have to undergo some trial or difficulty. That's the most basic of the irascible passions, or the most basic passion in the irascible power.

The flip side of that is fear. Fear considers what is evil. It represents a difficult evil that I don't think that I can avoid. Basically, it's something that's going to visit itself upon me, and I consign myself to my fate. I just cower in the corner and let it come. I might have a passing fancy or a small hope that it can be evaded, but I basically think that this is how this is going to go down. I'm thinking of the movie *A Quiet Place* when Emily Blunt's character is bloodied and about to give birth to her child, and she's in a bathtub, and these terrible creatures are stalking her. What do you do? If you make the smallest movement, they're going to do whatever they do. So she's riddled with fear because the evil that is threatening her seems, practically speaking, unavoidable.

Matt: It makes so much sense that these four principal emotions concern good or evil as either present or still in the future. If it's present, I love it if it's good or perceived as good, hate it if it's evil or is perceived as evil, or I hope for it if it's a good to be attained but is not yet present, or I fear it if it's an evil that could come upon me, again, whether actual or perceived.

Fr. Pine: It is indeed. Maybe some people think it's a little overly facile, but it's a helpful way of conceiving of it in very clear terms.

Matt: Fear flees from future evil, and hope strains towards future good.

Fr. Pine: Then again, to revisit the flip side, you have hatred, so the recognition of something out there as unfitting. If that thing is threatening or coming towards you, or if that thing is not yet present, it begets in you aversion. You want to shirk it. You want to draw away from it. You want to otherwise avoid it. But if it visits itself upon you, if it's something that you find unavoidable, then it begets in you sorrow or pain. In the most basic sense, St. Thomas will just talk about it as *dolor*, which we recognize from the word "dolorous." Then when it's a more spiritual resonance, he talks about it as *tristitia*, sadness, or the flip side of *gaudium*.

Related to that is despair. Basically, despair regards a good, but it's a good that you have effectively given up on. Every man who has loved a woman who is better looking than he is has had the experience of despair. It still regards the good because it's a consideration of her beauty, but you realize the disproportion between her beauty and your ugly mug, and that causes you a kind of sadness. It's not like fear, where it's an evil attacking you. It's not like she's haranguing you for being so homely. It's just that you're like, "Bummer. This good thing which so tortures and tantalizes my young twelve-year-old aspiring heart is inaccessible, and as a result of that I should go home and play video games," which is heartbreaking.

Truth be told, this doesn't need to have a moral color to it at the outset. I'll never be a good basketball player, and so I can despair of that, and that's fine, because if I were to try at this point in my life and given my vocation, it would be wildly disproportionate. If I were to spend three and a half hours in the back yard taking jump shots . . .

Matt: So despair in this sense doesn't need to entail a sort of emotion, because when you say you despair of not becoming an NBA player, you don't mean that you feel sorrowful about it necessarily.

Fr. Pine: Yeah, it's just an appetitive movement away from a good that you realize isn't going to happen. It can have a spiritual dimension, where it's a rational judgment of "no dice," but in its most basic sense it's a good you see and you know, "This won't happen, and I guess that's okay, or maybe it's not okay. I haven't yet reconciled myself to the fact, but I have to recognize it at the very least."

Matt: Let me offer two quick summaries of the emotions from Francis Selman in his book *Aquinas 101*. He says, "The emotions then are movements of our sensitive appetites when we apprehend things as good or evil." Then he says, "An emotion is a movement of the appetite felt as a result of the impression of something good or evil." If that's true, then if we encounter something that we perceive to be neither good nor evil, then we don't have an emotion, right?

Fr. Pine: There are certain things on offer that strike us as neutral. St. Thomas will say that there are no neutral moral acts because you always choose for a good or an evil end, but there are things in reality that don't move our wills or intellects.

Matt: If I scratch my nose because I have an itch, and I do it unthinkingly, this wouldn't be considered a moral or a human act. Right?

Fr. Pine: There are acts that are non-voluntary rather than voluntary or involuntary. It's not that we've chosen to do something in a profoundly human way or we've had it forced upon us, whether by coercion or fear or deep concupiscence, whatever it is. It's the kind of thing that our will doesn't even really enter into. The pumping of our heart, like you said, the scratching of your nose, these are things that just happen instinctually.

At least initially, emotions belong to a neutral encounter with reality, which is just another way of saying that the emotions on their own terms are neither good nor bad. What matters is how they are incorporated into a human life.

For example, when a river meanders, it gets more and more sinuous, but then sometimes the water just breaks through and cuts off one of the meanders. That, my friend, is called an oxbow lake. Let's say this river is torrential, so it floods the countryside in a way that makes the land fertile, but it's also super destructive. The emotions are like this. They're helpful for industry and trying to get things done, but they also can be really destructive. The virtues are like a huge dam, because then you can control the river, you can control its flooding, you can still use it for industry, you can still use it for transportation, you can still use it for agriculture, but you can actually use it better. You get hydroelectric power, and you're able to power the entire countryside.

Matt: So the virtues don't just repress the emotions, they channel them into something useful. Got it. Tell me, though, how Thomas' understanding of the emotions being good and, to some extent, neutral, helps us in our spiritual life?

Fr. Pine: If you were to ask most Christians, "Does man desire too much or too little?" I think a lot of people, based on their formation, would say that we desire too much.

Matt: We have to curb our appetite. We have to stop following all our inner desires and cravings.

Fr. Pine: Exactly, like we think too much about food and drink and sex, etc. Truth be told, the real drama of Christian life is to desire more or to desire better, and our passions are just the raw energy which supply us with the initial get-up-and-go to do just that.

For example, if you're often thinking, "Wow, I'm super irascible and angry. That causes me great concern and deep consternation," that's not a big deal. This is part of how God is saving you, because if you are vehement, if you are passionate, it's because God has a plan such that this is going to grow in you. It's going to be healed, it's going to be purified, but it's also going to be elevated. It's going to be inspired in a pretty profound way. I think that you're going to glorify God in a way that is vehement and intense and passionate, but in such a way that it's now virtuous because it's been incorporated into truly human culture in a true human life.

If, at least initially, you're like, "Wow, there are a lot of super destructive tendencies in my life. I have an addictive personality," okay, sure, that might be the case, and getting rid of habitual sin will be tough at the outset, but then think of how well and how tenaciously you can cling to good habits. Think of how good you're going to be at streaks, reading whatever spiritual work that you want to read every day for one hundred days in a row, or sticking to your commitment to pray the Rosary. Whatever has a dark underbelly can also have a beautiful promise of real sanctification or real growth in the life of the spirit.

Matt: It's like when corporate asks Michael Scott, "What are your biggest weaknesses?" and he says, "I care too much and work too hard" and then they just stare at him and he casually says, "My strengths are my weaknesses."

Fr. Pine: Sure, why not? The point I would make to people, though, would, be "Don't worry. This is an indication of how God is saving you." The only thing that Jesus destroys, the only thing that he takes away, is sin. Everything else, he elevates and perfects. Your passionate life is part of the story of how you are made to glorify God, and that's good news. To be a saint doesn't mean to run roughshod over the things about yourself which might cause you a bit of consternation or fear or whatever. It means discerning the ways in which, or being faithful to the ways in which, God is saving you precisely in and through those things.

* * * * * *

Emotions are important. Our ultimate happiness comes not just from being virtuous because this is our duty or something we clock into like a job, but because choosing the good genuinely makes us feel good. It's like how when you start a diet, you are happy because you don't feel miserable anymore from your old eating habits, but the new food doesn't give you joy either. But after a while your habits transform these activities so that food that once hardly raised excitement now brings a smile to your face.

The same thing happens in the life of virtue, which is why the *Catechism* says, "Moral perfection consists in man's being moved to the good not by his will alone, but also by his sensitive appetite, as in the words of the psalm: 'My heart and flesh sing for joy to the living God [Ps 84:3]'" (1770).

11.

WHAT TO DO
WHEN LIFE HURTS

No matter how good we have it, no matter how wealthy we are, or how many good friends we have, or even how holy we are, all of us will experience sorrow in this life. A couple of years into my marriage when my wife, newborn child, and I were living in Ireland, I experienced a great deal of sorrow. I was never diagnosed as having depression, but the symptoms were similar to what other depressed people experience.

Sometimes it felt like I had a mournful weight hanging around my neck. For many people, the sorrows we experience in this life can feel so overwhelming that we think we might break. Fortunately, St. Thomas Aquinas has several excellent insights into what causes sorrow and what we can do to endure it on our path back to the joy God ultimately desires for us.

WHAT CAUSES SORROW?

Aquinas, following St. John Damascene, lists four species of sorrow: anxiety, torpor, pity, and envy. We've already covered envy in our discussion of capital sins, so let's focus on the other three sources of sorrow and how Aquinas says we can overcome them.

Pity is the sorrow we feel at another person's misfortune. Even if something bad doesn't happen to us, we can still feel sad because we empathize with the person who is suffering. If they are a friend or family member, the pain can be much more intense because we find it easier to "be in their shoes." Pity isn't a bad thing if it moves us to compassion, but it can be bad if it leads us to find our happiness in other people's misfortune (what the Germans call *Schadenfreude*) or despairing for others and thinking they are beyond any hope for salvation in either this life or the next.

When it comes to anxiety, Aquinas quotes Damascene, who summarizes the essence of it well: "the dreaded evil gives rise to fear, the present evil is the cause of sorrow."[1] When we worry about the bad thing that might happen to us in life, we feel afraid, but when the bad thing hits us like a ton of bricks, it is then that we feel profound sadness, or sorrow.

About one-third of people struggle with constant anxiety. It can be a breeding ground for fear because we increasingly feel "boxed in" or trapped by threats or hardships in this life. On the other hand, anxiety can bring us sorrow as we mourn the existential cage of worry that has taken away our joy. Aquinas describes anxiety, therefore, as that "which weighs on the mind, so as to make escape seem impossible."[2]

Finally, Aquinas uses a word you might not have heard before but almost certainly have felt: torpor. He writes that you feel torpor "if . . . the mind be weighed down so much, that even the

---

[1] *ST* I-II, q. 36, a. 1.
[2] *ST* I-II, q. 35, a. 8.

limbs become motionless."[3] Torpor is a kind of sluggishness we feel when we're sad. While anxiety makes our nervous minds feel like a pinball machine, torpor turns them into the ruminations of a tree sloth that seems to take forever to move. Sadness in this case makes us tired, lethargic, and not willing to want to do anything in life because we ask, "What's the point?"

Aquinas says that "sorrow is a kind of flight or withdrawal, while pleasure is a kind of pursuit or approach; just as pleasure regards first the good possessed, as its proper object, so sorrow regards the evil that is present."[4] In order to counteract these sorrows, Aquinas recommends five treatments that keep us from destructively turning inward and reorient us to some good we can pursue that leads to relief and eventually a return to happiness. Specifically, Aquinas recommends pleasure, tears, friends, contemplation, and my favorites: sleep and baths. Let's take a look at each of those in turn.

FEELING BAD AND FEELING GOOD

I know it sounds kind of obvious, but if you are enduring some hardship and you feel really sad, pleasure or feeling good can be suitable remedy. Aquinas says, "Pleasure is a kind of repose of the appetite in a suitable good; while sorrow arises from something unsuited to the appetite. Consequently in movements of the appetite pleasure is to sorrow, what, in bodies, repose is to weariness."[5]

In other words, sometimes our sadness can be rooted in a thirst for pleasure. Just as sleep is the antidote to fatigue,

---

[3] *ST* I-II, q. 35, a. 8.

[4] *ST* I-II, q. 36, a. 1.

[5] *ST* I-II, q. 38, a. 1.

pleasure can be the antidote to sorrow. In many cases, we've poured ourselves too much into work, school, family, and even religious observances and not left anything for leisure. The twentieth-century Catholic philosopher Josef Pieper wrote a great book on leisure where he said, "Leisure is only possible when we are at one with ourselves. Possession of the beloved, St. Thomas holds, takes place in an act of cognition, in seeing, in intuition, in contemplation."[6]

Now, Aquinas is *not* saying you should become a flaming hedonist who washes away his sorrows with whatever you find in Vegas and think will stay in Vegas. We must make a distinction between *legitimate* and *illegitimate* pleasures, or pleasures that give us repose and refreshment from sorrow by invigorating our souls and pleasures that just distract us in life and end up making us feel worse.

We've all had the experience, perhaps, of getting something unhealthy to eat, falling onto the couch, and spending hours on end watching mindless entertainment. It may be distracting for a while, but when you're done, would you say you feel really refreshed? Or, to provide another example, scrolling through your Facebook feed or your Twitter feed for twenty minutes isn't going to restore you. That's just the digital equivalent of raiding the snack pantry.

So, what are some things you can engage in that can give you legitimate pleasure? For me, it would be going on a date night with my wife. It would be spending some time in silence, reading. For you, it might be different, and Aquinas admits that pleasure depends "on the part of the disposition of the subject,

---

6 Josef Pieper, *Happiness & Contemplation* (South Bend, IN: St. Augustine's Press, 1998), 63.

[so] any sorrow can be assuaged by any pleasure."[7] Once again, this isn't a license to do whatever you want, but permission to indulge in the unique, legitimate goods that make you happy, even if they aren't everyone else's cup of tea.

TEARS OF JOY

But sometimes we are hit with something really difficult, like a severe medical diagnosis or the loss of a loved one. We can't just go on a walk or have a good bottle of wine to make those sorrows disappear. In the face of these trials, don't be afraid to cry. Aquinas says there are two reasons this helps.

First, "a hurtful thing hurts yet more if we keep it shut up."[8] (I love that he says this because my mum said that to me when I was five.)

So don't keep the pain shut up inside. Have a good cry. Groan about it.

I think for many of us, maybe we've forgotten how to cry because we've gotten the impression that it's somehow a shameful thing (especially for men). But it isn't. So maybe spend some time alone listening to some beautiful music. Allow yourself to feel your feelings and don't be afraid to cry. It's almost as if when we cry, that pain, if you want to think of it in a material sense, dissipates through our tears.

This might be explained by the fact that tears shed because of emotional pain cause the brain to release oxytocin, endorphins, and other chemicals that are associated with the dulling

---

[7] *ST* I-II, q. 38, a. 1.

[8] *ST* I-II, q. 38, a. 2.

of pain and the elevation of moods. Biochemist William Frey has even shown that emotional tears contain more proteins than "irritant tears," or tears caused by things like onions.[9]

The second reason Aquinas says we shouldn't be afraid to cry or groan is "because an action, that befits a man according to his actual disposition, is always pleasant to him."[10] In other words, if we're feeling really down, and we've got to put on a happy face for people, we don't like that. That's not a pleasing thing. We like to be able to express on the outside what we're feeling on the inside.

Remember, sometimes God gives us suffering for the express purpose of perfecting us and it's okay to let God know that's a tough proposition. St. Paul tells us, "To keep me from being too elated by the abundance of revelations, a thorn was given me in the flesh, a messenger of Satan, to harass me, to keep me from being too elated." We don't know if this "thorn" was a person or possibly an ailment, but Paul does tell us, "Three times I begged the Lord about this, that it should leave me; but he said to me, 'My grace is sufficient for you, for my power is made perfect in weakness'" (2 Cor 12:7–9).

So if you're going through something right now, don't be afraid to cry and to groan and to turn to our Lord in that crying and groaning and say, "Lord, be my refuge. Be my shelter." St. Peter even tells us, "Humble yourselves therefore under the mighty hand of God, that in due time he may exalt you. Cast all your anxieties on him, for he cares about you" (1 Pet 5:6–7).

---

[9] William Frey, *Crying: The Mystery of Tears* (Minneapolis: Winston Press, 1985), 44.

[10] *ST* I-II, q. 38, a. 2.

A FRIEND LIKE ME

The third thing Aquinas recommends to alleviate sorrow is good friends. First, the pain that we experience often feels like a weight, and when we see somebody share that pain with us by being compassionate (meaning *co-passio*, to suffer along with), it alleviates that burden. Secondly, Aquinas says that when we see the sympathy of our friends, we know that they love us and this brings us pleasure.

I think that because of social media, we have this idea that we can somehow have one hundred or two hundred or one thousand friends. That's just not true. The British anthropologist Robin Dunbar believes that human beings only have enough brainpower to juggle relationships with 150 people.

This doesn't mean we can have 150 best friends but 150 people we interact with regularly, like coworkers, classmates, family members, and friends. Dunbar goes on to say that we devote two-thirds of our social time to an "inner core" of fifteen people, five of which get 40 percent of our social time (personally, I think you can only have about three close friends, but maybe that's just me—I'm envious of people who have a dozen of them).

We should remember, of course, that among our friends many of them are going through sorrows right now. They may even be keeping them secret in order to maintain "pleasantries" with us. When's the last time that we've given them a call?

Maybe we should call them today just to check in on them and see how they're doing. It demands a certain type of heroism, I think, to continually journey with someone who's struggling with depression or some sort of cross, because it can be wearying being with somebody who's continually suffering and continually telling us about their suffering.

So I think it does demand a type of heroism, not just to be there for the short term, but to consistently reach out to this person, to invite them out for a drink or to love on them, to allow them to share with you. I love what St. Paul says in his Letter to the Galatians: "Brethren, if a man is overtaken in any trespass, you who are spiritual should restore him in a spirit of gentleness. Look to yourself, lest you too be tempted. Bear one another's burdens, and so fulfil the law of Christ" (Gal 6:1–2).

CONTEMPLATING JOY

You and I aren't merely animals, so we shouldn't be seeking pleasure in the same way dogs and horses do, namely, through food or sex. We can certainly find these things to be pleasurable, but we can find even deeper pleasures when we use the rational abilities God gave us. We can raise our minds to contemplate the true, the good, the beautiful, and ultimately God himself, who *is* truth, goodness, and beauty.

Aquinas says intellectual pleasures are greater than bodily pleasures. I would have asked him, "Yes, but have you ever surfed in San Diego?" Obviously, I'm joking because I know the most beautiful experiences in my own life have come in the form of some prayer and it is in that spiritual vision that I've seen things of far more importance than I ever have with my physical eyes.

For example, in his discussion of pleasure, Aquinas recalls Augustine's observation that most people, given the choice between blindness or insanity, would pick blindness. We'd rather have our intellectual vision even at the cost of our bodily vision. Deep down we know that pleasures that penetrate the soul yield more joy than fleeting ones we sense in the body.

There is a momentary powerful joy of catching a nice wave, but there is a supreme, lasting joy that comes from acquiring the knowledge of surfing and knowing this is a part of your very being. There have been times when I've just lain on my surfboard, looked up to the sky, and said, "How good you are, God. How good you are for creating oceans and suns in all their beauty. How amazing it is that they faintly radiate your beauty!"

SLEEP IT OFF

The final antidote to sorrow Aquinas recommends is sleep and baths. Isn't that the best answer anyone's ever given you?

Aquinas quotes St. Ambrose, saying, "Sleep restores the tired limbs to labor, refreshes the weary mind, and banishes sorrow."[11] Against the objection that sorrow is in the soul whereas baths affect the body, Thomas replies, "The normal disposition of the body, so far as it is felt, is itself a cause of pleasure, and consequently assuages sorrow."

The body isn't a costume our souls wear on earth. It is a vital part of us and when it isn't functioning, that can have detrimental effects on the soul. It's ironic that in a time where we have more labor-saving devices than anyone else in human history, we are still so tired because we feel an incessant need to fill up our days and weeks with "stuff," lest we feel bored. In fact, one in three U.S. adults does not get at least seven hours of sleep a night (which I write as I hypocritically work on this book at one in the morning).

---

[11] *ST* I-II, q. 38, a. 5.

So, if you're of age, you might decide tonight to turn off all your electronics by 5:00 p.m. Don't have any more coffee after 5:00 p.m. Have a large glass of red wine, have a hot bath, and have a good night's sleep. And when you wake up in the morning, offer your first thoughts to God. Praise him because he is good, praise him because he loves you, and then maybe reach out to a friend who's not doing so well and remind him or her of the goodness of God.

12.

HOW SCRUPLES
STEAL HAPPINESS

AFTER THE BIRTH OF OUR FIRST CHILD, our family was living in Ireland and I remember feeling like God was always unhappy with me. I felt like I was walking through God's pristine, white-tiled kingdom and leaving dirty footprints and mud behind me everywhere I went. I thought God was looking for a reason to grab me around the scruff of my neck and throw me out of his kingdom.

Paradoxically, the thing that should bring me true happiness, my relationship with God, was actually making me miserable because I always felt like I was under some kind of divine microscope and never measured up. It turns out that I was struggling with something that many believers encounter as they pursue holiness and happiness: scrupulosity.

Medical professionals actually consider scrupulosity to be a variant of what is now called obsessive compulsive disorder. *The Wiley Handbook of Obsessive Compulsive Disorders* says this affects 10-33 percent of people with OCD, and these people have "excessive religious fears or doubts about sin . . . and committing the unpardonable sin, as well as fears related to confession, the Eucharist, and adequate articulation of prayers."[1]

The big questions that people with scruples struggle with are, "Am I in a state of grace? Am I in God's friendship, or did I do something to really make him mad and I'm doomed to hell for all eternity?"

AM I SAVED?

First, we must remember that salvation is not a moment that happens once in the past that forever determines our eternal destiny (a view common to many Protestants). For example, while St. Paul says we have been saved (past tense) by grace through faith (Eph 2:8–9), he also says we are being saved (1 Cor 15:1) and that we must work out our salvation in fear and trembling (Phil 2:12). Finally, he says "salvation is nearer to us now than when we first believed" (Rom 13:11), which implies that our final salvation lies in the future.

Instead, our salvation lies in becoming God's adoptive children and entering into friendship with God. So when Catholics wonder, "Am I saved?" what they really mean is, "Am I in God's friendship or a 'state of grace' at this moment?" The *Catechism* says, "All who die in God's grace and friendship, but still imperfectly purified, are indeed assured of their eternal salvation," but they will be purified after death through what we call purgatory (CCC 1030). But those who die apart from God's grace and friendship will forever be separated from him in the next life.

---

[1] Jedidiah Siev, Jonathan D. Huppert, and Shelby E. Zuckerman, "Understanding and Treating Scrupulosity," in *The Wiley Handbook of Obsessive Compulsive Disorders*, eds. Jonathan S. Abramowitz, Dean McKay, and Eric A. Storch, vol. 1 (Hoboken, NJ: Wiley-Blackwell, 2017), 527.

While we are in the body, our wills can be affected by our passions. We can choose the good, fall away from it, and then come to our senses and repent. But once the soul leaves the body, it isn't affected by the ever-changing nature of our passions, or bodily desires. Or as Aquinas says, "The soul is, of course, in a mutable [i.e. changeable] state so long as it is united to the body, but it will not be after it has been separated from the body."[2] The reason there won't be sin in heaven is the same reason there won't be repentance in hell: our wills will be forever "locked" in an orientation towards or away from God's friendship.

So how can we know if our souls are ordered towards God's grace and friendship *right now*? Aquinas says there are three ways we can know this.

First, we can know it by a special act of revelation, but that's pretty rare (you probably don't have a burning bush showing up outside church every time you go to confession). Second, you can know a thing by examining it with proper principles, but since grace isn't an earthly reality but comes from God and his free choice to bless us, we can't know we have his grace with this kind of inquiry. However, Aquinas says there is a third way we can know we are in a state of grace. He writes, "Anyone may know he has grace, when he is conscious of delighting in God, and of despising worldly things, and inasmuch as a man is not conscious of any mortal sin."[3]

When we talk about having certainty in our salvation, we have to distinguish between *absolute certainty* and *moral certainty*.

During the Protestant revolution, people like John Calvin proposed an idea that no one had ever believed in the previous

---

[2] Aquinas, *Summa Contra Gentiles*, bk. IV, ch. 95, a. 5.
[3] *ST* I-II, q. 112, a. 5.

1500 years of the Christian faith: once a person is saved, it is impossible for him to lose his salvation. This belief has been called eternal security, and it was condemned as a heresy at the Council of Trent, where it was called "a rash presumptuousness." The Council fathers declared in the decree on justification:

> No one, moreover, so long as he lives this mortal life, ought in regard to the secret mystery of divine predestination, so far presume as to state with absolute certainty that he is among the number of the predestined, as if it were true that the one justified either cannot sin any more, or, if he does sin, that he ought to promise himself an assured repentance.[4]

In other words, we can't say, "I will never fall from the state of grace," or "Even if I do fall, I am certain that I will repent before the end of my life." Only God has this knowledge because only God knows the future. We don't have "foreknowledge" of the future like God, but because we are created in God's image we have good old regular "knowledge" of the present. This includes knowledge of our souls and whether we are in a state of grace. This knowledge doesn't lead to absolute certainty like the certainty we have that 2+2=4, but it does lead to a certainty that guides our moral actions, like whether we need to get to confession or not (hence the name moral certainty).

DID I REALLY SIN?

When I spoke with Fr. Gregory Pine about our passions, he shared something with me that I think is very helpful for peo-

---

[4] Council of Trent, Decree Concerning Justification (1547), ch. 12.

ple who struggle with scrupulosity. I said, "I think a lot of people worry about tempting thoughts that can just kind of pop into their mind from nowhere, and they wonder if they've sinned just by considering them. What advice do you have for them?" Here was our exchange:

Fr. Pine: When it comes to temptations, there's very little you can do to stop them. You can manage the inputs and watch out for situations like drinking too much or watching suggestive media. But we must remember that the Lord permits temptations to arise so that your character can be tried and proven, and in the case that you do fall, that he can bring about in you a growth in the virtue of humility and a deepened recognition of your own dependence upon the Lord.

We are embodied creatures, so things that we recognize out there on offer are going to appeal to us. They're going to stir up our appetites, and they're going to move us. The question is what happens next. Is that something to which we consent? Is that something that we entertain? Is it something upon which we dwell? Or do we develop a prudence whereby we can dismiss those things or perhaps flee from those things or perhaps sideline those things?

People have all different kinds of ways of dealing with temptation. But that our appetites are moved should not in any way surprise or scandalize us. It will come. Gird your loins, and take up your staff.

Matt: I had someone come up to me the other day, and he was talking to me about these sexual daydreams that would come upon him. I've experienced that. I think most people have, too. Sometimes something like that will pop into your mind, and you wonder, "Oh gosh, was I just sinning there?"

This person was asking me, "How do I know when I've crossed that threshold and that this is now something I need to repent of, as opposed to, say, a fleeting thought?" What do you say to people who come to Confession and might have a question like that?

Fr. Pine: I would say to start with the act, and then back it up to what immediately precedes the act, and then back it up to the more remote culture that lays the groundwork for the act. With respect to the act, did you consent to it?

Matt: What does that mean? That's a difficult thing to figure out sometimes.

Fr. Pine: I don't think that it's an especially fruitful spiritual exercise to try to determine with each discrete act whether or not you consented because I think that that builds into your examination of conscience and to your discernment of your own interior state a kind of scrupulous spirit. Now, I'm not saying that we're dismissive and all wild and wooly about the matter, but I think that what we're ultimately trying to cultivate are virtues, and they're just more involved than taxonomy or the identification of specific, discrete acts. I think people suspect when it's happened, and I think at that moment you repent of it.

Matt: There's one thing if you discover yourself thinking about something. It's another thing if you say, "I'm going to spend the next little few minutes just thinking this through." That would be more the will.

Fr. Pine: I think people suspect that they have, and then they make an Act of Contrition, but then they try to dismiss the thought, because as with any sin, the next temptation is the devil's blackmail: to think yourself unworthy, to get down on yourself for having failed, which ultimately is a logic of self-reliance. It's like, "I ought to have done better. I ought to be better."

Like St. Catherine of Siena said, "Never think of your sins apart from God's mercy." That's not to say that we presume upon it, but it is to say that we acknowledge the fact, we repent of it, so you just make a small Act of Contrition, "Lord, I am sorry," but then you flee from it. You flee from the thought of the thing because that itself can now represent a kind of temptation.

UNFORGIVABLE SINS?

People who struggle with scrupulosity often think that any little misstep is a mortal sin, which is just flat out wrong.

Every time we go to Holy Communion, we're essentially saying, I'm confident that I'm in a state of grace. And this gave me a tremendous confidence. As my spiritual director said to me, "Matthew, when you come to Christ, when you accept his salvation, you are standing on a mountain, okay? And this mountain is not easy to slip off of. In fact, you can't slip off of it. If you want to throw yourself off of this mountain, you can, but that takes a free, deliberate, conscious choice."

And of course, what he's referring to is mortal sin, but that isn't something that we slip into. After reading *I Believe in Love*, which is a retreat based on St. Thérèse's writings, I came to see that my salvation consists of standing on a mountain with Christ holding me up and, unless I jump off that mountain willingly, I can have a high degree of moral certainty about my salvation.

First, the Bible says that the righteous man stumbles seven times a day—or more informally, "we all make many mistakes." These are venial sins that blemish our souls and hamper our relationship with God but do not destroy God's love in our souls or completely cut us off from God in the way a mortal sin does. For a sin to be mortal it must, as the *Catechism* says, be freely chosen, be grave or serious in nature (like violating one of the Ten Commandments), and you have to know it's a bad sin (CCC 1857–1860).

But what about the so-called "unforgivable sin"? The most terrifying verse in the Bible for a person who suffers from scruples is Mark 3:28–29: "All sins will be forgiven the sons of men, and whatever blasphemies they utter; but whoever blasphemes against the Holy Spirit never has forgiveness, but is guilty of an eternal sin."

Forgetting to keep your promise of saying your daily Rosary is not the "eternal sin." The *Catechism* says that the "eternal sin" Jesus is talking about is a reference to the sin of never asking for forgiveness for one's whole life. "There are no limits to the mercy of God, but anyone who deliberately refuses to accept his mercy by repenting, rejects the forgiveness of his sins and the salvation offered by the Holy Spirit" (CCC 1864). Aquinas says this sin "is said to be unpardonable, since in no way is it pardoned: because the mortal sin wherein a man perseveres until death will not be forgiven in the life to come, since it was not remitted by repentance in this life."[5]So if you're worried about seeking God's forgiveness, then you haven't committed an "eternal sin," since that's the sin of never seeking God's forgiveness for one's whole life.

---

[5] *ST* II-II, q. 14, a. 3.

DOES GOD LIKE ME?

According to support groups like Alcoholics Anonymous, one of the greatest lies an addict believes is, "If you really knew me you wouldn't love me. You wouldn't stick around. You would know that I'm not worth it." But to know Christ is to know that's false. To know Our Lord is to know that I'm loved and I think that's the truth that we have to accept.

But I think many of us still think, "God loves me but he doesn't like me. Or maybe he loves me in an obligatory sense like the way I'm supposed to love my parents, but he doesn't delight in me." I think that is what I struggle with and I think that a lot of the time the root of this is scrupulosity. In fact, it can be hard to believe God loves us when saints we already think are "perfectly pious" are the ones who tell us about God's love.

When I was a kid, my mum would affirm all of my drawings, anything I did, like "That's great, Matt." But it didn't mean much. But when dad said it, I thought, "Wow, that must have been good." Likewise, when a saint known for flowery devotional language like, "God is just dripping with mercy for you," I say, "Yeah, yeah, got it." But when Aquinas soberly tells me, "It is a false opinion that [God] refuses pardon to the repentant sinner or that he does not turn sinners to himself by sanctifying grace," I feel relieved. Someone is just telling me the truth—he isn't trying to merely make me feel better in light of my inadequacy.

Aquinas goes even further and says that "despair, which is in conformity with [this] false opinion about God, is vicious and sinful."[6] The person who falls into despair because he thinks his sins are too great for God to forgive actually thinks God is

---

[6] *ST* II-II, q. 20, a. 1.

too small. While in a state of prayerful ecstasy St. Catherine of Siena dictated this private revelation from God, "My mercy is greater without any comparison than all the sins which any creature can commit; wherefore it greatly displeases Me that they should consider their sins to be greater."[7]

Meditating on this was really helpful in addition to just sitting before Our Lord. And one of the prayers I used to pray when I was going through this was, "Lord, would you tell me that you love me until I finally believe you? 'Cause I really don't believe you." And sometimes maybe it's because we're so familiar with the language of "God loves you" that it's an impediment to growing in our understanding of God's love.

Another problem for people with scrupulosity is that sometimes we compare our relationship with God to our relationship with other people. We know our relationships with other people can be destroyed through single, major acts of betrayal or by many small annoying and insensitive behaviors. So we think that our daily sins must eventually make God so mad that he wants nothing to do with us anymore.

First, while God is infinitely more merciful than any human being we know and love, our human relationships can still reveal, even in an imperfect way, the goodness of God's love.

For example, when you're dating someone, you might fret at the beginning of the relationship about whether it's going to last. Does she like me more than I like her? Do I like her more than she likes me? Did I do something that's going to torpedo this whole thing? But I've been married for years, so I don't think that anymore. I'm not trying to have control over my relationship and the love my wife has for me. I *submit* to her

---

[7]   Dialog of St. Catherine of Siena, A Treatise on Prayer.

love; I don't need to fully understand it.

And what's lovely is that, although my wife can go back on her promises because she's only human, God can't do that. Scripture tells us, "God is not a man, that he should lie" (Num 23:19). God isn't subject to the irritabilities that haunt our human relationships. Our constant minor faults can add up to major "breaking points" for some people, but when it comes to venial sins, Aquinas says that the idea that many venial sins can equal a mortal sin is false because "all the venial sins in the world cannot incur a debt of punishment equal to that of one mortal sin."[8]

God's mercy and grace are infinitely beyond our human failings, which is why we have confidence in our salvation. That confidence comes not because of our purely human efforts, but because of God's unfailing divine love. Or as Peter Kreeft puts it, "We can be sure God will never abandon us. We cannot be sure we will not abandon Him. Our faith is in Him, not in ourselves."[9]

When St. Thérèse was on her deathbed, the sisters said to her, "It's no wonder that you're so confident of Heaven, we don't think you've ever committed a mortal sin in your life." And she said, "It's not because of my lack of mortal sin that I go to God with confidence. Even if I had committed all of the sins imaginable I would still be this confident because I know that all of my sins compared to his mercy would be like a drop of water flicked into a raging furnace."[10]

---

8 *ST* I-II, q. 88, a. 4.
9 Kreeft, *Practical Theology*.
10 Quoted in Jean LaFrance, *My Vocation Is Love: Therese of Lisieux* (Homebush, Australia: St. Paul's, 1994), 75.

Thérèse is *not* saying that God doesn't care if we commit mortal sins. She is saying that God's mercy that we receive when we confess our sins to him is so powerful that we should let it envelop our fears, concerns, and neuroses about being forgiven and replace it with his peace.

You can believe that God doesn't like you and he won't have mercy on you. You're welcome to do that. You can also believe that the world is flat. That's fine. But I invite you to reality. And sometimes I think that Christianity, or at least my relationship with Christ, is just the long story of Christ refusing to believe me when I tell him I'm not worthy of his love.

CONCLUSION

HAPPINESS, WITH A LITTLE HELP FROM AQUINAS

Reading St. Thomas Aquinas is a bit like reading Shakespeare; it's confusing because we aren't used to the language, but once we get the language, the beauty shines through to our souls. So yeah, you could watch a reimagining of *Romeo and Juliet* like *West Side Story* and get the basic understanding of the plot, but if you do that, you lose the beauty of the original text that can be found in lines like, "My bounty is as boundless as the sea, My love as deep; the more I give to thee."

I'm not saying it's wrong to use a study guide or popularization of either Shakespeare or Aquinas. In fact, most people should do that in order to understand the text. I'm just saying that if you stay there, if you only read summaries of the texts, then it's like restricting your diet to fast food and missing the intricate dish the master chef has been making.

In this book you hold in your hand (or hear in your earbuds), we've only scratched the surface of what Aquinas has to teach us.

So, if you want to read Aquinas for yourself, especially the *Summa Theologiae*, I recommend reading a summary of the chapter you want to explore so that you know the basic idea that Aquinas is talking about. You can find these summaries online on websites like *aquinasonline.com* or in books like Peter Kreeft's *A Shorter Summa*. Then, you can go through Aquinas' own writings in order to really appreciate his wisdom and fine-tuned arguments. But in order to do that it will help to know how Aquinas writes, because it's not like the books you're used to reading—and here's why that's a good thing.

THE BIG PICTURE OF THE *SUMMA*

There are a lot of topics that are addressed in the *Summa Theologiae*, and if you've listened to *Pints with Aquinas* for a while, you've probably seen me address some pretty crazy questions and wondered how they all fit in the *Summa*. For example, I've done episodes on topics like "Are wet dreams sinful?" and "Is it a sin to get drunk?" The answer, of course, is yes to getting drunk, and no, it's not a sin to have a wet dream (but you can go back and listen to those episodes to find out why).

We've done other episodes on some pretty far-out topics, and so you might be wondering, how on earth does this all fit together? Well, it is actually very structured. Peter Kreeft explains it this way:

> The structural outline of the *Summa Theologiae* is a mirror of the structural outline of reality. It begins in God, Who is "in the beginning." It then proceeds to the act of creation and a consideration of creatures, centering on man, who alone is created in the image of God. Then it moves to man's return to God through his life of moral and religious choice and culminates in

the way or means to that end, Christ and his church.[1]

So, as Kreeft says, it starts with God and then it goes to God's creation of man, then it focuses on man. Then it focuses on man's return to God. And then it focuses on what is man's return to God. Well, it's through Christ. And so that's when it starts focusing on Christ and his Church, which is the way back to God. So you can think of it like a circle.

You start with God in the first part, which also talks about creation. Then, you move to man in the second part, Christ, the sacraments, and the last things in the third part. These are the three basic parts of the *Summa*, all of which are divided into treatises, which are kind of like chapter headings covering distinct subjects in each part, like "the Incarnation" or "the Cardinal Virtues." Then things get really interesting with the questions that make up each treatise and the articles that make up each question.

So it goes part, treatise, question, and then article. Stay with me, because when Aquinas uses these words, they differ slightly from how we use them. For example, what we mean today in English by "article" is essentially an essay. If someone says, I wrote an article, you assume they mean they wrote an essay of sorts. But when Aquinas refers to articles, he means question.

So to give you an example, we've been talking about the second part of the *Summa* (which deals with man). There is a treatise on cardinal virtues and question seventy-three is simply "of backbiting." As you see, it's not really a question; it's more of a summary of the questions Aquinas is addressing on the subject.

---

[1] Peter Kreeft, *A Shorter Summa* (San Francisco: Ignatius Press, 1993), 153.

Basically, backbiting, or detraction, is the unjust damaging of someone's reputation by truthfully revealing that person's faults or sins. A lot of times we justify gossip by saying, "Well, what I said about him was true, so what's the big deal?" It's true that calumny, or the spreading of lies that hurts someone's reputation, is sinful, but so is detraction. A good way to remember the difference is that the L in calumny stands for lying and the T in detraction stands for the truth. It's wrong to spread lies that hurt reputations, but it's also wrong to spread truths other people have no business knowing that hurt people's reputations.

When it comes to this issue, Aquinas lists four articles, which are really just questions related to detraction:

(1) What is backbiting?
(2) Whether it is a mortal sin?
(3) Of its comparison with other sins;
(4) Whether it is a sin to listen to backbiting?

THE *SUMMA* IN ACTION

Before we look at one of these articles as an example, let me explain the nature of the articles so that it's easier for you to read them. Each article has five parts: the question, the objections, the *Sed contra*, the *respondeo*, and then finally Aquinas' responses to the objections. As I mentioned before, I love that Thomas starts by acknowledging the toughest objections to the position he is going to defend. They're kind of a preview of what he's going to refute later, but for now they help set the stage for his explanation.

He begins by asking a question, and the question is always formulated in a yes-or-no format, such as "whether God exists?"

So you can think of the *Summa* as a summarized debate just like how we have academic debates today where there is a question or resolution (e.g., Does God exist? or it might be stated "Resolved: God exists"). There is somebody who argues for the proposition and someone argues against it, and in St. Thomas' time people believed that we could discover truth by dialectic, or through conversation with another (couldn't we use more of that today?).

We live in what we might call an epistemological relativistic society. That is to say, many people deny that truth is even knowable at all. Maybe truth is just relative to individual people, but if truth does exist, we can't really know it anyway. But that wasn't the case in St. Thomas' time. And so, for that reason, the medieval scholastics thought of debate as a sort of science or an art form. If you compare what Aquinas does in the *Summa* to the absolute train wreck of "Presidential debates" we've had in the U.S. in recent years, you'll see what I mean.

Today it's not really about getting to the truth. It seems to be about either showing who is the most clever, or who has the "mic drop" moment. But the other extreme are people who say, "Let's agree to disagree and no one's really right, no one's really wrong, it's just our opinion. We should respect all opinions equally." This is ridiculous because not all opinions are equally true (some are complete rubbish).

So after the question, which for our purposes we can take from the second article on backbiting, "Is backbiting a mortal sin?" you have the objections. Aquinas usually tries to come up with at least three objections to the position he holds, which in this case is, "Yes, detraction or backbiting can be a mortal sin." The objections go as follows: 1) a virtue can't be a mortal sin and it is virtuous to denounce a brother's wicked behavior.

2) Proverbs 24:21 says everyone suffers from this vice and a behavior can't be a mortal sin if everybody does it; it must be venial. And 3) Augustine said it was only a venial sin.

As you read through the objections in the *Summa*, it's easy to get confused because some of them aren't made anymore, but they often reveal attitudes people hold today, and any of the objections are just as relevant today as they were in Aquinas' time. If they confuse you, just skip them for now, and focus on Aquinas' reasons in the next part of his answer, the *Sed contra*.

This means "On the contrary," and here Thomas offers a short argument from authority, or the basic response from the Church to this objection. He might quote what the Fathers of the Church had to say, or the saints have had to say, or Sacred Scripture to get the essence of his reply. So in this case he appeals to the writings of St. Paul and says, "On the contrary, It is written (Romans 1:30): 'Backbiters, hateful to God,' which epithet, according to a gloss, is inserted, 'lest it be deemed a slight sin because it consists in words.'"

But Aquinas doesn't stop there.

He then gives the *respondeo* ("I respond" or "I answer") and offers a defense of the teaching. In this case he says, "It is a very grave matter to blacken a man's good name, because of all temporal things a man's good name seems the most precious, since for lack of it he is hindered from doing many things well."

Aquinas then heads off several objections by noting that the revealing of faults is sometimes justified in the service of a necessary good (such as by warning people of an escaped criminal's crimes and his violent nature). In other cases faults are revealed carelessly like when you have "loose lips," and this is a venial rather than a mortal sin. But if your desire is to destroy someone's reputation just because you want them to be reviled in the eyes of others and not for any "necessary good," then the action involves grave matter and can be a mortal sin.

Finally, Aquinas rounds up the objections and dispatches them one by one. First, it's not a sin to reveal faults if the purpose is good, such as to help someone amend their life, which is virtuous. It is mortal if the purpose is primarily to harm their reputation, usually out of a malicious motive, so this act is not under the virtue of charity. This also relates to the citation of Augustine, who was talking about inadvertently revealing faults, not the full-on sin of detraction. Finally, the passage in Proverbs the critic cites only says detraction is widespread, not that it is universal or that everyone engages in this sin all the time, which would be more becoming of a venial sin than a mortal one.

KEEP GOING!

It seems like many Catholics today and many evangelicals are making a virtue out of doubt. Now don't get me wrong, doubt can be helpful. There's no use in pretending you believe something. If you don't believe it, then you doubt it, and therefore you ought to ask questions in order to gain certainty. Because here's the thing: if God has revealed it, then there's no humility in saying, "What do I know?" I'm giving up certainty, and making a virtue out of skepticism in that sense. Rather, if we do doubt the Catholic faith or if we do doubt elements of it, then what we should do is formulate a question and pursue the answer. But we're not going to be able to pursue the answer unless we first know the question.

Another thing we can learn from articles, which has to do with the *Sed contra*, is the need to understand what the Church's position is on these things. And one of the best ways to do that is by reading the *Catechism of the Catholic Church*. I'm always surprised when I pick up the *Catechism* by how rich it is and how much I learn from it.

We've been exploring happiness, and, guess what? The *Catechism* has a whole section on Christian beatitude. It says in part, "The Beatitudes reveal the goal of human existence, the ultimate end of human acts: God calls us to his own beatitude. This vocation is addressed to each individual personally, but also to the Church as a whole, the new people made up of those who have accepted the promise and live from it in faith" (CCC 1719).

In the same way, there is a whole section on the virtues that allows us to go deeper and learn how to apply that knowledge in our lives. So when somebody says, "Faith is just wishful thinking," you can say that glorious "*Sed contra!*" (well maybe to yourself, so as not to be off putting): "On the contrary, the *Catechism* says, 'Faith is the theological virtue by which we believe in God and believe all that he has said and revealed to us, and that Holy Church proposes for our belief, because he is truth itself'" (CCC 1814).

Faith isn't believing something because we want it to be true; faith is trusting in a revelation because it is true.

We can apply this same way of thinking not just to matters of doctrine, but also to matters of morality and, in particular, to the virtues we need to live out in order to be truly happy. We live in a world that pays lip service to virtues but is also quick to say that temperance or prudence are just "repressive thinking" and that faith and hope are "religious fundamentalism." It's easy to lose our confidence when people attack our way of life and seem to be as happy or even happier than we are. That's why it's good to do the hard work to get the reasons, like the one Aquinas uses, to justify our path to happiness.

We've seen Aquinas' ultimate source of happiness. Surely it wasn't wealth, which he renounced through his religious vows. It couldn't have been pleasure (what hedonist drives away a prostitute with a burning iron?). If Aquinas were seeking happiness through power, he would have spent more time positioning himself among the elite than preaching, teaching, and writing. And honor? Even if Aquinas desired praise, say, for his intellectual accomplishments, doesn't the end of his life speak to his detachment from success and renown? Who among us, recognizing the worth of our work in the grand scheme of God's majesty, would not continue laboring to prove our salt?

The roomfuls of books authored by St. Thomas Aquinas— great good that they were and are—were utterly meaningless in the shadow of a brief moment of union with our Lord. And that's Aquinas' secret. Of all his brilliance, that's the one thing Aquinas would leave for us: *"Nothing, if not you, Lord."*